STRIPPED

49 LIFE LESSONS LEARNED FROM DYING

ALSO BY NANCY MICHAELS

Perfecting Your Pitch (2004)
Career Press Inc

Off The Wall Marketing Ideas (1999)
Adams Media

Media Madness (1997)
Impression Impact

A to Z to Visibility (1997)
Impression Impact

How To Be A Big Fish In Any Pond (1996)
Impression Impact

Copyright © 2013 by Nancy Michaels.
All rights reserved.

This book or any portion thereof may not be reproduced or used in any manner whatsoever without the express written permission of the publisher except for the use of brief quotations in a book review.

The names of those included in this book have been changed, to protect the innocent... or guilty.

Printed in the United States of America

First Printing, 2013

ISBN-13: 978-1940678009

Impression Impact, Inc., PO Box #1288
Concord, MA 01742

www.nancymichaels.com

TO ERICA MULLINS STEWART
(1984 - 2005)

*whose life was tragically taken
to miraculously save mine*

CONTENTS

Acknowledgements	ix
Prologue	xiii
Chapter 1: Waking Up is Hard to Do	1
Chapter 2: Rise from the Ashes	27
Chapter 3: Just Breathe	69
Chapter 4: Who Says You Can't Go Home?	85
Chapter 5: That's What Friends Are For	109
Chapter 6: Homeward Bound	141
Chapter 7: Where the Boys Are	157
Chapter 8: Love Hurts	173
Chapter 9: When You Wish Upon a Star	187
Chapter 10: Back In the High Life Again	209
Epilogue: Gifts from Being an Organ Recipient	223

ACKNOWLEDGEMENTS

I f "no man is an island," then certainly no book has ever been written single-handedly. This is certainly the case for **Stripped**.

My heartfelt thanks and gratitude -- first and foremost -- go to the story I have been blessed to have bestowed on me. I am truly grateful for such a tumultuous start to my fifth decade -- although, not by choice -- it has taught me so much about survival, the will to live and greater compassion for others and myself. I would never wish the life-and-death circumstances I endured on anyone, nonetheless, it occurred to me, and I believe, I am a better person for it.

Huge thanks go to my amazing team including Monaica Ledell, Barbara Remillard, Kim Sutton, Chela Hardy and Barbara Holsombach, who have made huge contributions to this book and at times, were far more passionate and encouraging about it's "birth" than I was. They also were key in helping me to edit, re-write and re-organize the content. I could not have done this without you.

Thank you also to Susan Frasca and Josephine Scanlon, the Duet Write team, who listened to endless hours about my separation, illness, divorce and recovery to help me jump-start this creation. They were patient and truly instrumental in helping me express my jumbled thoughts and get them on paper -- or the screen. My overwhelming gratitude to both of you.

There are no words to thank the people who were there to support me through this re-birth, as well. My parents, Tom and Cathy Staiti, my three brothers, Tom, David and Peter, along with their amazing wives, Darlene, Lisa and Melissa -- I cannot thank them enough for being with me every step of the way, through what was a harrowing process.

My children, the three angels who will always be my babies -- who, thankfully, still have their mother, and whose love is the most unconditional love I will ever know. They inspired me to live on and fight to get back to them. They were, and truly still remain, my inspiration.

Special thanks to my colleagues who are in my mastermind group(s), including -- Marilee, Marc, Stacey, Brian, Jeff, Jill, Angie, Jim, Nicholas, and Joshua, who are so encouraging and supportive of me, my business and this book. We are kindred spirits and it's nice to feel so comfortable with my "peeps." I am thrilled to have you in my social, personal and professional network of supporters.

My friends who believe in me, sometimes more than I believe in myself, including -- Sandy, Glynne, Carolyn, Norah, Barbara, Jeanne, Margaret, Roberta, Michelle, MJ, Linda, and Robin.

My special friend, Tom Steeves, who helped to launch me in a new business endeavor and has assisted me every step of the way. I'm so glad to know and love you, and have you as my partner.

My past and current clients -- from both big and tiny companies, that have kept me on my toes and entrusted me to represent them, on their behalf -- my extreme gratitude.

PROLOGUE

death

/deTH/

Noun

The act or fact of dying or being killed; the end of life of a person or organism.

May 23, 2005

    That was the day I died. It was the day I left my old life behind. It was the worst day of my life. And the best.

"We must see all scars as beauty. Okay? This will be our secret. Because take it from me, a scar does not form on the dying. A scar means, 'I survived'."

- Author Chris Cleave

CHAPTER 1

WAKING UP IS HARD TO DO

My body screamed at me with a medical malfunction so bad that the consequences would strip me naked of everything important in my life.

Nevertheless, I did not hear -- nor heed -- the warning.

In hindsight, my swollen body was a glaring symptom of a frightening health problem. All I saw that particular day, however, was that I needed those pants to fit, damn it.

No amount of lying on the bed, squirming, writhing and sucking in my stomach would wiggle me into a pair of jeans that suddenly became three sizes too small. I needed magic pills and the newest mega-whatever diet to revamp my body that was so bloated it looked like I was trying to squeeze 10 pounds of shit into a five-pound bag. That's not stretching an analogy as much as you might think, either.

What the hell had happened? What were these imposters, posing as my jeans? When was the last time I had worn them? Was I going through menopause? Did I need to give up carbs -- completely?

That was wake-up call No. 1. It was the first warning that my body was turning against me. Unfortunately, I didn't hear the warning. I'll bet you're thinking you can relate to a pair of pants being too small, but I hope not for the reason I had. I wouldn't wish the type of alarms my body started setting off on anyone. Well, maybe the old me would have wished them on my worst enemy, but that was before July 17, 2005, when I finally woke up, in more ways than one.

The events of my life leading up to that fateful day consumed me: I had grueling separation and divorce proceedings, after nearly 20 years of marriage; a terrifying judge who initially heard our case; attorneys, who made a bad situation far worse -- all while I tried to raise my 6-, 7- and 9-year-old children and build my business.

I was feeling really run down. With all that was going on, I knew I had not been taking great care of myself and needed to get back into the swing of things. So, being newly single and wanting a change, I decided to join a gym. Isn't that what every 40-year-old woman does, who is looking for a new lease on life?

Since I've always been what some might call an overachiever, I attended a variety of training sessions -- cardio, weights, Pilates -- to kick it up a notch.

Yes, I hated it -- like most women, when they first start working out their bodies, after a long hiatus. I loathed all those skinny young girls hanging around, who worked off the stick of gum they just chewed. But, I didn't let that stop me. Since there was no magic pill to get me back into shape, I knew it was all up to me. Time for some tough love.

So tough that I nearly fainted and threw up during a weight-training session. I just lay down on the floor in the middle of the gym, unable to help myself. One of the employees took my blood pressure, which had spiked to 140/120, more than 20 minutes after the incident. I was advised by the gym powers-that-be not to come back, until I'd had a stress test. If you think that's embarrassing and humiliating, you ain't heard nothing yet.

For two decades, I had been a successful consultant in business development, sales and marketing, and helped others build their business enterprises. I was traveling around the country writing books and designing CD/ROM training courses, as well as speaking in front of business groups, chambers of commerce, trade shows and conferences -- and enjoying it all. Life had been good. I was a published author and had a client roster of A-list, Fortune 500 companies. My husband, Matthew, owned a successful business that had been in his family for several generations. I was living a great life -- or so I thought. More accurately, so I told myself.

When I met Matthew in college, he was a skinny 25-year-old, who looked more Blue Blood than Jewish. He had straight light brown hair, a straight nose and some of the fairest skin on the planet. Within a short period, after our first date, we got married and began an upwardly mobile, acceptably "happy" life together.

Then, at age 40, which I had considered a meaningless milestone as it approached, when I thought life would only get better with my career established, a lovely home in the Boston suburbs and my kids coming along nicely, my husband of 16 years said he wanted out. Honestly, it didn't quite come as a shock. I think many people go through life in a marriage just as I did. I was working at living life to its fullest, despite the problems. Which means, basically, ignoring the problems and focusing, instead, on what's good. In other words, you sweep things under the rug -- all too often. I certainly did, and fell prey to the material goods that surrounded me. I felt I should be grateful for the things, regardless of the emotional "expense."

All the while, our marriage had been like a leaky faucet draining the goodness out of our relationship, one drop after another, never ending -- *ping, ping, ping.* The drop that led to the flood that devastated our lives, was that Matthew found love with a woman named Kim. She was a "licensed day care provider," according to his court affidavits. Little did I know what a saving grace it would be, ultimately, to me,

Matthew and most importantly my children, that this woman had entered our lives at this critical juncture. As I reflect back on that seemingly endless period of life-and-death struggle that ensued, I am grateful that Kim was there for our children, when I couldn't be.

What I did know was that Matthew and I had been "enjoying" the perks of a 16-year relationship: a nearly sexless marriage, his participation and interest at an all-time low, along with a huge home on top of a foundation that was literally crumbling from water damage, in our basement. All this was the physical manifestation of the mold and decay symbolizing what had become of my marriage.

Think Edgar Allen Poe's "The Fall of the House of Usher," where everything about the home is representational. Our home was indicative of the slow dissolve of a union built on an unsteady foundation.

My home was ripping at the seams. So was my marriage. The same for my heart. Apparently, the rest of my body didn't want to be left out of this whole mess, hence the episode at the gym. Atlas himself couldn't have shouldered the stress I was enduring. Now, I needed a stress test for my body. Go figure.

While the thought of seeing a doctor to get the not-so-skinny on my health was less than appealing, I was feeling progressively weaker and nauseous. I knew there had to be something serious going on with me. I took a series of stress tests and couldn't even walk the treadmill for two minutes before they pulled me off. The initial diagnosis was high blood pressure, and medication was prescribed as treatment.

If that diagnosis was correct, then what was happening in my life was unlikely to make that condition any better. My attorney's son had attempted suicide during my divorce proceedings and, understandably, his head was not in the game. My new attorney, for whom I borrowed a $10,000 retainer from friends, did not appear to be putting up much of a fight for me, either. I came to learn that his wife was suffering from ovarian cancer. Feeling pained for him, but also feeling undefended and pretty much left for dead myself, I sought a female attorney, who came highly recommended. The third time proved to be the charm, although by that time, I was so sick that I didn't think I would even make it through my first meeting with her. However, I did.

After several trips to my primary care physician and X-rays at the local Emergency Room, the doctor decided that I probably just had the flu, maybe bronchitis. During my first Mother's Day as a single mom, I vomited the entire weekend -- such a lovely way to spend the day. My nine-year old daughter, Catherine, played mom to me and made macaroni and cheese for herself, her little brother and sister. The following Wednesday, still feeling awful, I forced myself to go to the Emergency Room at Emerson Hospital, where some blood was drawn for testing. I spent all day in divorce court on Thursday -- the last case of the day, as I ran back and forth to the bathroom the entire time. My parents came with me and by day's end, I tossed my heels and walked with stockings all the way back to the car, waiting to get home and climb into bed once again. So, it probably wasn't the wisest decision to take a flight to Atlantic City on Friday for a speaking engagement. My blood pressure was still very high, but how could I know my body was undergoing organ failure? The doctors didn't.

I have only fractional memories of that trip about which to speak. It, basically, went like this: got on the plane, puked, got off the plane, puked, checked into the hotel, puked. Apparently, I called my mother to tell her that I had made the trip safely, but have no memory of doing so.

I tried to rally, wanting only to complete my two sessions and run -- Okay, crawl -- back home. However, the only running I could do was to the planter in the ballroom. Great way to make an impression on a roomful of people; those weren't quite the pearls of wisdom falling from my mouth for which they'd signed up.

Life Lesson #1:

They say you always feel better after vomiting. I sure didn't. When you find yourself puking in front of a roomful of people, who paid for the privilege of hearing you speak, it's time to go home.

I could no longer fool myself that this was just a bad bout of the flu, and I'm not ashamed to admit that at this point, I prayed for a miracle.

My miracle was waiting to pick me up at the airport in Boston -- J.C. She was my neighbor, a Realtor, and a friend, who on that day was also my savior. Hailing a cab would have been beyond me. You learn a lot about who your friends are when your life starts falling apart.

Life Lesson #2:

Ask for help, even from new friends. They often end up becoming among your closest friends, because of you reaching out to them in a time of need, when they respond with kindness. It also makes people feel good to know that you think enough of them to ask for their help or contribution to your well-being.

You know you're in deep shit, when you voluntarily elect to go to the Emergency Room on a Saturday night. I dreaded it, but crazies or not, I knew I had to go. So began a mind-boggling array of medical mysteries and horrors that would come to rule my life for the next year.

I was admitted to the hospital through the Emergency Room that night. My parents were contacted, and arrived early the next morning on May 15, 2005, just before I was transferred to Beth Israel Deaconess Medical Center in Boston -- to the Intensive Care Unit.

Although I vaguely remember that transfer, I do recall thinking how gorgeous everyone was upon my arrival at Beth Israel; as if I had been transported to the set of the television show, *Grey's Anatomy*. I wasn't yet grasping the severity of my situation, since it didn't have an actual identity yet. Being newly single, I was looking for Dr. McDreamy. All I got was Nurse McQuestions.

"What have you done in the last six months?"

Puke.

"What did you do in the last month?"

More puke.

"Have you been with anybody intimately in the past week?"

What? Right, because all men find vomiting highly sexy. Here, let me show you.

"Have you been out of the country?"

Yes, years ago when we adopted our two daughters in China. More puke.

The questions were never-ending, and it suddenly felt more as if I was on an episode of the dark television show *House* than *Grey's Anatomy*, when the Infectious Diseases Department came to visit. I began to understand why people admit to crimes they didn't commit -- as a way to stop the interrogation and torture. Enough already. I have no clue why I look like the Pillsbury Doughboy and am sick as a dog. Please just fix me!

My belly was swollen and hard by this time, and the consensus was that I was in kidney and liver failure. No one could isolate the cause, hence the interrogation. About two or three days into my stay, they discovered that my kidneys, in fact, were functioning, though my liver was not.

The hits just kept on coming. May 19 ranked right at the top of the charts. It's a date I'll never forget. Having a surgeon tell you that you need another person's liver surgically transplanted into your body ranks right up there with birth, death and your wedding day.

"Nancy, you're going to... we have to do a liver transplant." My head was spinning, my mind racing, as I heard the voice of my surgeon, Dr. David Hanson. Was he really speaking those words to me?

A transplant? Doesn't that mean I need a donor? Wait. What the hell are you talking about?

I just kept thinking, *"This can't be happening."*

In a matter of three days, I went from Atlantic City to the Emergency Room to the Intensive Care Unit. I went from thinking that I knew what was important in my life, what I wanted and what I needed to do, to knowing little or nothing about my own life and having no ability to do anything about it.

Of course, I didn't know it at the time, but I was put into a medically induced coma, which says something about the severity of my medical condition. I had no concept of what was going on in my own room, let alone in my life or the world-at-large. The visuals became varied patterns of light, sounds protruded, voices faded, and the smell -- a very distinct septic and sterile odor -- was the only way I could recognize my location. In retrospect, maybe it was a blessing. At least I wasn't able to be actively terrified, while waiting for a new liver, in a coma.

I do have vague memories of people being in the room and looking at me or talking to me. A friend says I squeezed her hand; however, I can't recall that at all. I do know that the machines in the room would go crazy when someone came in -- which, I understand, demonstrated that I was more or less aware, on some level. My mother was panicked as she heard and saw my heart monitor increase and was concerned that she shouldn't come in because it was too upsetting. Thankfully, a sweet young nurse assured her she should continue to come in.

It was nearly two months before I was actually aware of the presence of someone in my hospital room. On July 14, the doctors reduced the medications that kept me under, and three days later, I became aware -- well, semi-conscious -- of my surroundings for the first time in a long time, a weird feeling, further distorted by all the drugs that remained mercifully in my body.

As I shifted my eyes to look at the clock, I was able to comprehend that it was 7:13, though I was unsure if it was the morning or evening of July 17th -- thanks to the calendar that was posted on the wall. That's a feeling to which anyone can relate, who has taken an overnight, red-eye flight.

Other than the eerie whispers and the unnerving sounds of the overwhelming number of medical devices and machines that surrounded me, the room was amazingly still. Something at my core told me I had not taken a red-eye. I wasn't in Kansas, Dorothy.

I wish I could say that my awakening was one of those miraculous and magical moments, when I opened my eyes surrounded by family and friends (including my remorseful husband), smiled at all of their concerned faces and realized how beautiful and precious life really is. Cue the angelic chorus in the background.

But, no, it wasn't that kind of awakening, though with the gifts of time, blessed with humor and people I knew, I eventually would see the light at the end of one very long, dark tunnel -- figuratively speaking.

When I opened my eyes from that two-month-long coma, the revelations I did have were purely delusional. The hallucinations I experienced, largely due to the medications I was taking, are a story unto themselves. The Cliff Notes version is this:

One time, I believed I'd found the cure for cancer and quickly slapped my buzzer to try to alert the staff with my muddled thoughts for a cure. Another time, I thought 80 sets of twins, that were going to be adopted, had been eaten by a pack of security dogs, instead. The newscast, in my warped mind, was previewing what was happening in the world and I believed I could help stop it in some way. I also believed the nursing staff was stealing my medications and plotting my death, because -- of course -- it made perfect sense for them to knock me off, after they'd worked so hard to save me.

Did I mention that I woke up with a tracheotomy, or trach, a surgically implanted tube running through an opening in my neck and into the trachea (the windpipe) to help me breathe? I was seriously suicidal, too. I couldn't imagine living like that. I couldn't speak. I couldn't ask questions. I just wanted to scream -- but I couldn't. With everything that was happening to me, I had zero voice, which I guess went well with my zero dignity.

Doctors assigned a psychiatrist to me, after my physicians realized I was in a brutal state. It seemed a fairly ridiculous idea. With the tube still down my throat, I couldn't utter a shred of my concerns. So, what was the point?

There were efforts at communication along the way, such as the lip-reading episodes. My brother was the best at reading my lips; my mother was terrible at it; and then there was the woman who would come by to read my lips and try to tell my family what I was asking. It was one of the most frustrating experiences of my recovery.

Day and night were filled with nothing but anxiety. I hardly ever slept. The night shift typically did the bathing around 2am, and blood work came around 5am -- forget the machines that went off continuously and kept me up all on their own.

Then, lucky me, I had a sweet nurse who was learning to play the flute. What better audience than someone drugged, gagged and bound to her bed? Not to brag but I had been first flutist in my high school orchestra, had many private lessons and had even been touted by one teacher as the Kenny G. of the flute world.

What this nurse was doing was an assault upon my ears. I'm sure she thought she was helping, even relaxing me, while I thought that she'd be a great form of extreme torture for terrorists and criminals. Night after night she practiced the same tune, "Edelweiss." Since my kids were huge fans of *The Sound of Music*, I was painfully aware of the soundtrack of this film and let me tell you, she was not helping my recovery one little bit.

On my last night of musical blasphemy, my favorite nurse, Margaret, told me the flutist would be staying with me overnight. I erratically shook my head no -- the only way I could effectively communicate my displeasure. Margaret got the message and relieved the flutist. Though I suppose I should have felt badly, I had some deviant thoughts about what she could do with that flute. Since I couldn't act on them, I was simply relieved.

Because of the strong medications I was on, I was convinced that my Asian nurse was my ex-husband's girlfriend, Kim. She was really a very sweet nurse and it gave my neurotic mind peace to know Matthew was going to marry such a nice girl. Really?

She'd sit with me for hours while I'd fill myself up with anxiety. My eyes darted and shifted around, waiting for the next attack of killer nurses. She stuck close by and even helped to eliminate the funk from my trach tube (she specialized in respiratory care). Yep, Matthew was going to marry a wonderful girl. Thank God, for my children's sake. I would often try to express my gratitude to her -- despite the trach. She must have thought I had lost my mind, which -- of course -- I had.

I remained delusional and dependent for what seemed like ages. At one point, I even turned on Frederick (the wonderful male nurse who had taken such great care of me since the day I was admitted) thinking he also was attempting to kill me. My mother had initially objected to a male nurse for me, but even she had a serious change of heart and Frederick had now become the house favorite.

Some memories, unfortunately, were all too real. Anne, the nurse, who every day after I woke from the coma put me in a Hoyer lift (a hydraulic powered sling device that allows patients to be transferred between a bed and a chair) that caused me so much anxiety. I'd defecate everywhere before they were ready to crank me up. The humiliation of losing control of your bodily functions should only happen *after* you've lost your mind -- as it wouldn't matter much then, would it? I felt extreme embarrassment and shame for the literal mess I had created, though Anne couldn't have been more kind.

"We'll clean you up, Nancy. Don't worry." She explained to the male nurse's aide that I got anxious just before being lifted and that it was a common occurrence. However, I had to have been on her "shit" list. Who could blame her?

I came out of my coma panicked, petrified, and delusional -- similar to the way I went into it.

Imagine thinking you've got some fiendish form of the flu one day and being told you're in organ failure the next. Imagine going from waiting for a liver donor one day to waking up an unimaginable, unlived 60 days later. Or, imagine going from being a strong woman surviving a wicked divorce and raising kids, while still building a successful business, to being emotionally shattered and physically near death.

There were so many questions going through my head. I was in shock for hours, probably days, trying to focus and process what had happened to me, while I was sleeping in a coma.

Life Lesson #3:

Sometimes, it really is true that ignorance is bliss. Television show CBS Sunday Morning reported of late that "no time is wasted if you're sleeping." I couldn't agree more.

I didn't have the flu. I had suffered renal failure, a liver transplant and, oh yeah, brain surgery. Doctors told my family that I had been on -- and off -- a donor list. At one point, a compatible liver had become available but it was a male's liver and probably too large for my body. Then, I was yanked off the donor list because the odds were that I probably wouldn't even survive a transplant. Friends and family later told me that my father was unable to accept this as an option and continued to ask the same question over and over. *"When she gets back on the list, how long will it take for you to find her a new liver?"* The doctors explained repeatedly that I wasn't on the list, as it was unlikely I could survive the surgery.

I was told that visitors were asked to leave my room on several occasions because my heart rate would shoot up and I appeared anxious. Apparently, there were conversations in my room, with me lying right there, about the possibility of me not finding a compatible donor. I'm guessing my body reacted to that negative energy. You think?

My poor parents -- I can't even imagine strapping in for the roller coaster ride that they were taking. I'm not sure how I would handle the stomach-churning, bottom-dropping-out feeling if I had to face the same ordeal with my own children. Prior to my transplant, the doctors determined that it would be necessary to perform cranial surgery -- drilling a hole in my skull to alleviate the pressure on my brain. Unfortunately, it did nothing to alleviate the pressure on my parents and brothers. They had the misfortune of observing the aftermath of this procedure and I believe they still suffer post-traumatic stress from that.

As devastating as all of this was to my mother, when the hospital tried to have last rites administered to me, she would have none of it. She told them no. It wasn't my time.

Life Lesson #4:
I now know that I never want to hear last rites -- although I probably would have taken the bait at the time -- and that wouldn't have been a good thing. What an excellent call by my mother.

After the cranial procedure, I still needed a liver and the doctors put me back on the donor waiting list. Unfortunately, organ donation is done by region and New England is one of the most difficult areas to get an organ. Maybe it's because of the area's low crime rate and fewer vehicle accidents, which would normally make it a desirable location. However, my life was anything but normal.

Doctors made the decision to expand the search for a new organ while I was lying in a coma. The sad fact was that someone else would meet a tragic fate for me to find a liver. I still would be alive because someone else was not -- yet another thing I was not aware of until months later, after "waking up."

It was my oldest brother Tim Jr. who told me the story, post-transplant, of the 21-year-young woman from Virginia who died May 21. She had been in a car accident and was Med-Flighted to a Tennessee Hospital. She was a mother, like me. Her life status changed in an instant, like mine. I didn't know how sick I was; she didn't know her own life would be cut short. She would be my savior but her two young children would lose theirs. My heart broke for her and her family; every breath I drew devastated me about her life ending.

I can't imagine the strength it takes to see a loved one dying and, before their last breath, make the decision to give someone else a chance to live. To love so much you want to hold on as long as you can, yet have the courage to say goodbye and let go. To selflessly give someone else, a stranger no less, the chance of life while your heart is breaking at the thought of never again being with the person who is your very heart and soul.

A young woman died. I was one of the lucky ones who lived on through her -- because of her. This one woman saved more than one life that night. We are many who owe our lives to her last act on this earth.

Sunday, May 22 was the day of my transplant surgery. It didn't finish until the next day and not before I flat-lined twice. The second time I "coded" was the most critical, when the surgeons discovered my new liver contained a blood clot. In the early morning hours of May 23 I was lifeless on the operating table for a full two minutes. The organ had to be taken out, the clot removed, and the liver checked for other clots, before being replaced. All of this while my heart was stopped and then rebooted, much like Windows software on a computer, except they use paddles in the Operating Room.

To this day the memories during that near death experience swirl in my mind. There were no white lights or calming voices during my extended emergent surgery. Despite what I now know -- I'm sure there were -- along with a stellar medical team.

Instead, I felt I was "elevated" and hovering over myself on the operating table. The bright lights were coming from the operating room fixtures that focused down on my open body and me.

I had thought I was undergoing surgery to remove parts of me so I would look fabulous on the cover of a magazine. Do you remember when Oprah was on the cover of *Vogue*? I think that's what prompted this idea in my mind. I always loved Oprah and was so thrilled for her to make the cover. Come on! Might I be operated on to lose those extra pounds for, perhaps, the cover shoot of *Boston magazine*?

The pain was the most excruciating I had ever experienced -- how could that not be real? The only kind of pain I had ever tolerated -- as many women have -- was when I gave birth to my son and had been put on Pitocin after the doctor had broken my water. Heavy labor instantly occurred -- paling pain in comparison to what I was experiencing now.

In my mind I pleaded with the Operating Room team to stop and just let me go -- I could no longer take the pain.

A nurse continued to tell me, *"You'll be ok -- you're almost done."* My pleas to stop the cutting continued and her response was always the same.

I think I said, *"I don't really care if I look good, just let me die!"*

After my endless begging to be let go, I heard the voice of my youngest brother Paul, helping me to convince the stoic nurse that it was too much and to please let me go. She insisted it would end soon. Therefore, it must have.

Something propelled me from being pinned in that most painful dream to an even more painful reality -- and still unable to move, speak, or do much of anything but hallucinate.

Many have told me "I'm here for a reason." I certainly hope so, but in my endless begging to die in those moments -- something I've never conceived of and wouldn't have wanted to occur unless the pain was so overwhelmingly unbearable -- I still remain hopeful.

The doctors had concerns that I had suffered cognitive damage due to prolonged loss of oxygen to my brain; they informed my parents that I might not be *the same*. I am here to tell you that those doctors were right. I will never be the same, but it has nothing to do with my intellectual ability to absorb facts and knowledge. It has everything to do with a change in my perception of what is meaningful and valuable in life. On the forefront of the change in my perceptions -- I believe I've nurtured what's important in my life quite well.

One thing about waking up from a comatose state, realizing you have a shaved head, I.V.s shooting out from your limbs like the tentacles of an octopus, drains in all kinds of places in your body and a trach tube crammed down your throat -- it tends to give you a perspective you can't get from anywhere else.

Apparently, I took about a month too long to wake from my comatose state. Being a patient in a teaching hospital means you're a learning experience for interns -- a living textbook for those students, if you will. That's nerve-wracking enough but July is when the new interns start their duties. Those folks were in for a real treat with me as their new patient. On the other hand, I was lucky to have survived.

Life Lesson #5:

Never be so sick that doctors admit you to a teaching hospital in the month of July.

I was told that within one week of my transplant surgery, back in May, I had a pulmonary infection and aspergillums (a fungal infection in my lungs) due to my nonexistent immune system. The fungus includes many common molds, which makes me wonder about my previous wet and moldy house. Naturally, my lung problems were an exceedingly rare occurrence but I suppose I am just one of those exceptional people. I did mention that I'm an overachiever, didn't I?

Within two weeks, after my transplant, while performing a routine CT scan (a Computerized axial Tomography that combines special X-ray equipment with sophisticated computers to produce detailed, multiple images of the inside of the body) of my brain, my doctors found a cranial abscess. I am nothing if not a challenge. They took me, immediately, back into surgery after an emergency phone call to my parents to obtain their permission.

Since my husband had continued our divorce proceedings in the midst of all my medical trials and tribulations, he was not the person to consult about any treatment options for me. Therefore, my poor parents not only endured all of the emotional pain of seeing me so ill but made all of the decisions regarding my care, as well. Between them and my wonderful neurosurgeon, at least I knew my life was in good hands.

I should mention that I re-assigned my parents to be my health care proxy that would have otherwise defaulted to Matthew -- something people should know to do if they don't want their current spouse to be calling the shots while they're ill.

Well, I didn't actually know anything at that point -- thankfully, I was sedated throughout all of the breakdowns my body was experiencing. Nevertheless, I'm certain that I felt it.

After finally opening my eyes in July and after struggling through the hallucinations, one of the first questions I asked my parents was, *"Where is Matthew?"* I just assumed that he would be there. I could not imagine that he wasn't there after all the years we'd spent together, after all we'd been through together, after all we'd meant to each other and our shared roles as parents to our three amazing children.

Then, I was told that while I had been in a comatose state, Matthew pursued his custody battle for our children due to the severity of my medical condition. He had convinced a judge to give him legal and physical custody because he thought I would die. What I didn't expect was that he would only once bring our children to visit me and that was only upon my insistence to see them. Who am I? I am their mother! Hadn't he ever heard something about not kicking a person when they're down? Apparently not.

That's when I knew I had to wake up even more. It wasn't one of those "aha" moments of enlightenment. It was more like having hit snooze on the alarm one too many times -- and finally realizing it was time to wake the hell up.

When I first woke up, I saw a young female doctor come in to check vitals, write notes on the extensive charts that were posted to the wall, and when she turned around -- I nearly scared her to death. She composed herself and came closer to me, asking the standard questions. Did I know where I was? What year was it? Who was the president? Etc. Soon thereafter, a crowd of doctors and interns came to observe the circus lady that was me.

I had to fight with every ounce of courage in me. I had to fight for my life. I had to live for my kids. They needed me and I needed them.

My ex-husband's court actions to get my children gave me strength, when what I really wanted was to just give in and let go. In the end, it was the realization that he was taking away from me the one thing I needed most -- my children. If I could just get better and get out, I would get them back -- on my terms.

The people and things most important to me would always -- come first. I was resolved to survive my near-death experience so I could rebuild my life and remodel myself in the image I wanted to be.

Want the recipe for a completely new outlook on life? Try this: take a little pain, add a dash of sorrow, toss in one slice of a sorry liver and marinate it all in a 60-day coma. Voila! I promise you, you won't ever look at life the same way again.

Okay, maybe the ingredients in my recipe for making every day count are a tad extreme. I'm just learning to cook. But, as a wise man once said (and does anyone really know that it was a wise *man* who actually said this?) nothing in this world is worth having if it comes easy.

A wise Nancy, after traveling to hell and back, couldn't agree more. My life is living proof. So is yours.

CHAPTER 2

RISE FROM THE ASHES

You've heard this before and I will say it again and again and again -- if you don't have your health, you truly have nothing.

Until my health crisis, however, it was my separation and the divorce that were the most difficult times I had ever gone through. Divorce is like a death but in some ways more painful because the connection with your former partner goes on, especially when you have children together. How do divorced couples manage that connection? That's the tricky part.

Although my ex-husband might never believe this, I am actually very grateful to him in many ways. The most obvious take-away from our relationship are three wonderful children -- first, our two daughters, who he never blinked an eye at adopting from China. I thank Matthew immensely for my daughters -- and our miracle surprise son, who was born into our world between their adoptions.

I desperately wanted to be a mom and the times I am with my children are really some of the best moments I ever experience.

I'll never forget getting the call from the adoption agency saying they wanted to meet with us the next day so we could see the photo of Catherine -- our first gift from China.

We met with our social worker, Jillian, and she handed the folder to us that had the most adorable photo of an infant baby girl. This sweet baby had a concerned look on her face that would become so familiar to me. She had a round face (like a moon) and her eyebrows furrowed, which showed her concern. She was wearing a hand-knit blue sweater. She was delicious and I was in love, as was Matthew. We went for Thai food for lunch and dropped the photo off to have copies made, to send to our extended families. I laminated one that I carry in my wallet, to this day.

It was excruciating to wait the few weeks before making the journey to China to meet Catherine, along with 21 other families, to meet their new baby (or toddler) daughters. I busied myself with creating the most amazing nursery in our home with a theme of the Cow Jumped Over the Moon. I had a friend of mine paint a clouded sky on her ceiling with baby cherubs, including a Chinese one. Too cute.

My in-laws bought Catherine's furniture -- to die for -- very feminine and just adorable. We never anticipated that the extreme feminine ambiance of the room wouldn't exactly match Catherine's personality as a baby and toddler. As it turned out, it was perfectly fitting for her and her personality down the road.

I was like a kid in a candy store when it came to baby specialty stores such as Gymboree, along with the baby sections at major department stores. This baby had a killer wardrobe and she hadn't even arrived.

I found a boutique clothier at a baby show and bought the most adorable pink outfit with top, pants and matching hats. I bet there are more photos of Catherine wearing hats than any other baby on the planet. I was obsessed.

Meeting Catherine, finally, was like leaving my body. Matthew and I arrived in China and toured for a few days with other families who were adopting. We met our little ones at our hotel. The Chinese adoption workers brought up one at a time -- right to our floor, off the elevator. We were holding signs up with the names of our child in Chinese. I think Matthew and I were near the end when a short woman with a friendly face came toward us, passed Catherine into my arms and said, *"Mama. Mama."*

Catherine took one look at me, her little lower lip started to quiver and she began to scream. Our precious baby was not happy.

This woman (her caretaker from the orphanage -- or so we thought), encouraged me to walk her. We asked questions with the help of our interpreter.

"What does she like to eat?"

"What time does she go to sleep?"

"Does she take naps? How long and when?"

The woman's responses were astounding.

"This baby goes to bed at 7 and this baby wakes up at 7."

"This baby has two, two-hour naps a day, from 9 a.m. to 11 a.m. and 1 p.m. to 3 p.m."

"This baby likes to be happy; this baby doesn't like to cry."

Okay, this was too good to be true -- but it was all true with Catherine AnYing Lilly Greenberg.

At one point, her caretaker, who had placed Catherine into our arms, took her back out of mine and began to sob into that blue sweater of hers. It was heartbreaking. Awful. It was so sad that I could hardly process it.

Her caretaker encouraged me to allow Catherine to sleep. She went over to her crib, made a clucking sound with her tongue and touched Catherine under her chubby chin. Catherine smiled up at her. I longed for that to be her reaction to me some day.

It was clear to me that they had a close personal connection about which I might never learn the real story.

Catherine was a dream baby -- she did exactly as her caretaker described. She went to bed at 7 p.m., she woke up at 7 a.m. -- never crying -- just cooing until I came in and she'd have a big smile on her face. She melted my heart and that of her father.

She was amazingly well taken care of, seemed plump and healthier than most of the babies who were adopted on our trip. I felt that she, at some point, was breast-fed and was rooting for me to feed her. The first day was awful, as she didn't drink a single bottle. By Day 2, Matthew and I had cut the nipples of the bottles, as advised. We were thinking she was propping, bottle-fed, like so many other orphaned babies. Catherine was not like the other babies, though. She guzzled that bottle down and we were too inexperienced to know this was NOT a good thing. Within minutes, while I tried to burp her, she projectile vomited into Matthew's suitcase. Thank God for laundry service in China.

To immerse Catherine in water for a bath was a new experience for her, as we soon discovered. She was petrified when we tried to bathe her after our third night with her. She had little black rings of coal in her creases -- that were everywhere on her body, including her belly button. At first, we put her in a tub and she arched her back in protest. She would not be having any of it. The second time, I got in the tub with her and she seemed better. By the time we got to Japan (on our way back to the States) she was loving her baths. After we were home I'd put her in our kitchen sink and she would go crazy splashing. What a transition.

Arriving home with her was so thrilling. She was the gorgeous little face on the evening news, wearing that amazing outfit. At the airport, the media (as well as family and friends) met us. They wanted to meet the newest members of all the respective families who had adopted in China. I was on Cloud 9 with Catherine – perhaps, one of the happiest years of my life. Of course, having a biological child between the two adoptions, and my first year with our second child from China, Savanah, ranked right up there, too.

As the saying goes, things happen when they're supposed to happen. A month after we brought Catherine home I had the great good fortune to be introduced to Roberta, a retired crossing guard, who was looking for a job. A mutual friend had suggested that Roberta might help with my business but she became so much more than an office assistant; she became a friend to me and a grandmotherly type nanny for my children. Thanks to her loving disposition and great skill, my kids never had to go to day care; Roberta took care of them while I worked on my consulting business, and later, when they came home from school. She is truly a blessing to my family (and the closest person I ever had to a wife). The separation and divorce proceedings were tough for my kids. However, my getting so sick while Matthew and I were separated seemed like an unfair much-too-heavy burden to put on our three young children. I don't know that I'll ever comprehend the full impact on them until they're older.

A few months later I can remember driving Catherine somewhere and looking in my rear view mirror, thinking how lucky I was to have this baby as mine -- my daughter. She was my little doll and I dressed her to the nines. I was frequently stopped with her at grocery stores and while walking through town by people who wanted to know where she was from or where I got her that hat or outfit.

Life got even more curious when I realized (after just dropping off our application to adopt again and Catherine was only 14 months old), that I was pregnant with Nathan. We were a real conversation piece. So many people told me that once you relax, you'll conceive. That was true for many of us but sadly, not for all. However, as an adoptive mother I couldn't feel more connected to all three of my children, including the two conceived in my heart.

Catherine was always a deep thinker. She'd pretend not to listen to you but she took in everything. She's also very resourceful and smart. An example of that occurred right after we brought Savanah home. Nathan was almost age 3 and Savanah was 8 months old. Matthew took them to the grocery store and it was snowing. He was contemplating how to get the three of them into the store, given their tricky ages.

Catherine piped in, *"Daddy, I know. Get out of the car, lock the doors and go get a cart with a baby seat. Put Savanah in the baby seat and Nathan in the back of the cart, and I'll hold your hand."* Matthew realized she had evaluated the situation and came up with a very logical solution.

One Friday afternoon I was hosting some neighborhood friends and their little ones when one boy slammed the sunroom door on Savanah's thumb, almost taking it off. I felt like I was going to faint. My friend, Lani, was telling me to get a pack of ice and socks and I was frozen in place. Seconds later, Catherine brought me her socks and a Ziploc bag full of ice. She remains calm and graceful under pressure.

That is until she went to Kindergarten -- and suffered severely from a chronic case of pediatric eczema. It was awful. Dentists would ask her if she had poison ivy, as well as retail sales people and others questioning what caused her skin condition. Her classmates were brutal -- never asking her over for a play-date at their house -- despite my taking days off to facilitate her having friends over to our house. She wasn't invited to one single birthday party of her classmates -- during the entire year. It was heartbreaking. So much so, that as a five-year-old she would wake up screaming at her skin and telling us she wanted to die or kill herself. She ended up spending time at Boston Children's Hospital the last week of school with what the doctor said was the "worst case of pediatric eczema" he had ever seen.

That's when I asked Catherine what her favorite school had been, of the different pre-schools she attended. She said, *"That cooking school,"* meaning Waldorf -- one of the kindest, most loving and nurturing environments a person could experience. She repeated her kindergarten year and remained at Waldorf until the eighth grade, when she acted as

Master of Ceremonies during her commencement. I was so proud and grateful she had this experience after such a harsh start in school.

The week that we decided to submit our application to adopt again, I was so thrilled. I had completed the paperwork to return to China. I bundled Catherine up on a cold gray day (it was November), and drove to Waltham to the adoption agency to meet with our agent, Jillian, and show Catherine off to everyone.

Later that day I felt light-headed and nauseas. I asked Roberta, our nanny, if she could stay while I took a nap. She agreed and after she left my nausea continued. I called Matthew and asked him to pick up a pregnancy test. He did, but we both doubted it would garner a positive response.

At first, I was annoyed at the more than $20 price tag for the test. Surely, that would buy Catherine another hat -- which she didn't need. I tossed the test on the table and left it there until the next morning. I had been pregnant before but had a devastating miscarriage. Therefore, I knew the feelings of being pregnant. When I woke up, I heard Catherine cooing in her room and went to the kitchen to retrieve the test. I peed on the strip and within seconds I saw the blue line that showed I was pregnant. Oh, my God -- you have to be kidding me. I told Matthew before he left for work. We were excited and hopeful -- but not like before, because of the miscarriage. It was good that we had our adoption application turned in and had already become parents with Catherine.

I called my doctor and the prenatal appointments began. The first ultrasound showed two sacs. I nearly fainted. I was expecting twins. After all that happened to us as a family, we were having two babies at one time. What would we do? Should we let the adoption agency know? *"No, sit tight and wait to see what happens,"* my gut kept telling me.

At the next appointment, a test showed that only one of the fetuses was viable. Was that disappointing? Yes, but in some ways it was a slight relief because it was so confusing. We still wanted to return to China. However, with three children under age 2, that might have been impossible. We would have to slow the process down a bit, as compared to before with Catherine.

The pregnancy turned out to be just fine. There was no drama around the other fetus being lost. Apparently, my body absorbed him or her.

I got bigger, enjoyed my coffee flavored shakes, tuna sandwiches and other comfort foods like macaroni and cheese and baked potatoes. Life was good -- it was more than good in so many ways.

I was thrilled to be with Catherine when curious people, who wanted to know my pregnancy story, stopped us to ask questions. It was a miracle that through infertility (or, so I thought), came the most beautiful gift of my Chinese daughter Catherine. I also was having the experience of being pregnant with a biological child. Oh, and there was another baby on her way from China. With three children, we would be done!

While I was pregnant, Matthew and I moved into a Currier and Ives kind of house on the other side of town. Sounds nice, right? We thought it might be, but looking back, I think the house is slightly haunted and we would have been better off staying put. I'm not sure whose idea this was and we probably would have differing opinions now on who, ultimately, wanted to make the move.

Honestly, in hindsight, the wear and tear on the marriage started to show after the financial hardship of the move, along with having two babies on the way and already taking care of one.

I noticed Matthew was not coming home on time and not calling to tell me why he was late. I remember one night when I was about five months pregnant and folding laundry in the kitchen (our laundry room was right off the kitchen). He came home -- obviously angry. We started to argue. I was upset he hadn't called. Looking back, he clearly was under a lot of pressure from something. He threw one of our kitchen chairs against the wall, which made a hole in the wall and broke the chair.

A few weeks later, I remember having his parents come over and they asked what happened to the wall. I simply said that Matthew was angry. Not good, and it was a sign of bigger things to come.

When I was ready to deliver Nathan (his due date was July 4 -- a real firecracker), I went in for a final check up on July 3. My doctor was concerned that I didn't have enough amniotic fluid and said I should go to the hospital after going home to retrieve my things. I called Matthew to tell him they were going to induce labor for me and then called my mom and grandmother Nonna to see if they could stay with Catherine.

I drove home and then drove myself to the hospital after my mom and grandmother arrived. Was there something wrong with this picture? I think so, now. Matthew continued to work and showed up at the hospital after work. I was on the drug Pitocin to induce the labor but had no major pains -- yet. The plan was to begin Pitocin again in the morning and break my water, so Matthew went home that night and was to return the following morning. I slept for a while and was awakened at 6 a.m. I took a shower, then then called my husband to say they were putting me back on Pitocin and were going to break my water. Two hours later -- in complete and full-blown labor and after being asked repeatedly by the nurses if my husband was coming -- I called my house again and my mother answered. I could barely speak, since I was in the throes of major contractions. I asked to speak to Matthew and I knew my mother could sense the upset in my voice. Matthew was eating breakfast and talking to my mother and grandmother. Really? Later I learned my mother was furious but would never have said anything to Matthew at the time. Big mistake.

Finally, he arrived. I was not pleased. At the same time, I needed help getting an epidural, an anesthetic injection into the epidural space in my spine to relieve pain, and getting to the bathroom. I got a Demerol dose instead, also for pain, which was like putting a

Band-Aid on a 9-inch incision. Finally, I received the epidural, which allowed me to rest. However, I wasn't fully dilated to give birth. Matthew was chit chatting with the nurses until the time came for me to deliver and I was told to push. The epidural was a relief but I only felt it on one side and below the waist. After about 23-plus minutes of pushing, my Nathan came out. Matthew was videotaping the events and his birth was such a miracle. They took all of Nathan's "signs," and he seemed perfectly healthy. He was/is -- just the way we hoped.

Catherine was in love with her new baby brother, who she would call "handsome boy," imitating what I would call him -- or "buddy." Too cute! She came to the hospital and Nathan had a "baby" doll to give her. After the nurses gave Catherine her own diaper bag with real diapers, bottles, etc., she instantly became my little helper.

I came home the next day and began planning a bris, a circumcision ceremony performed on an 8-day-old male by a mohel (a person in the Jewish faith trained to do the procedure). This was not easy for me. I called my friend to cater the event, got invitations out the door and pulled my house together for the family and friends who would attend as witnesses.

I couldn't bear to be in the room when the mohel did the circumcision. It seems barbaric to me but I had agreed to raise the kids in the Jewish faith (ultimately, that never happened because I didn't feel compelled to drive that train). My mother-in-law and father-in-law came to help, and they did. They also got me a baby nurse for several days after Nathan's circumcision -- which was a Godsend. Matthew questioned how I was taking care of Nathan's wound when I was all the while too weak in the knees to change him -- and I was in the midst of undiagnosed post-partum depression.

It was terrible and in hindsight, I'm shocked that someone didn't recognize my upset and ask me to seek help. I spoke to my obstetrics/gynecology doctor about the depression but she said it was "normal." It wasn't. I was crying constantly, all the while knowing that there was something wrong with the way I was feeling. I should be thrilled about my baby -- beyond thrilled. What was my problem? I had everything I wanted -- a beautiful baby girl, and now I had given birth to a handsome baby boy. Shut up, Nancy, and keep going.

I was excited when my mom and grandmother offered to come over and watch Catherine and Nathan for me so I could get out of the house. I took the afternoon to buy regular underpants again, not maternity, and had a peaceful lunch with no one pulling on me. It was heaven.

I was in a panic about going anywhere with the two babies. I remember waking up one Saturday morning (Matthew worked on Saturdays) and taking Catherine and Nathan to Whole Foods -- just to see if I could maneuver the double stroller I purchased after Nathan was born.

I had gone to the mall with Roberta, when Catherine took off in the food court and I was left sitting with Nathan. I was unable to move much due to the episiotomy (a surgical incision that was performed in the hospital at the time of Nathan's birth). I was fearful that the incision would tear open with any sudden movements. Suffice it to say, I really needed the double stroller now with a newborn -- and a 22 month old who loved to run off.

To make matters worse, we had purchased a tiny cottage-style house in Eastham, Mass., near Orleans and Wellfleet on Cape Cod. Sounds idyllic, and it was a lot of fun with just Catherine, but it was lonely, even then. I didn't have any friends there.

My parents would visit and Matthew would come down on weekends but it was very isolating. It was brutal after Nathan was born. I felt guilty for not using the cottage more. When looking back, we should have rented it out and stayed in our main residence in Concord, Mass. In Concord, I had a support network and could have gotten some help from Matthew during the nights when Nathan would wake up several times. It was an incredibly trying summer.

As time when on, I began to ask Nathan's pediatrician more questions about his development. Most people agreed that I was just a nervous new mother and boys developed more slowly, when I compared him to Catherine.

Three months after his birth I could sense something was very off with Nathan. He cried constantly -- unless I was holding him or he was placed in a bouncy chair in front of the television (something I never would have considered with Catherine). With him up at least three times a night, as well as me suffering from postpartum depression, physical and emotional exhaustion, I was in a major funk.

As my network of friends with small children grew, I was learning about PDD (Persuasive Development Disorders) and ASD (Autism Spectrum Disorder) from them. Making friends with mothers of small children was easier after giving birth to Nathan, because adoptive parents don't have a group of people they travel with to doctor's appointments and such. My inner beliefs about Nathan seemed to have much more merit, as my talks about these topics continued with my friends. I was referred to a woman who lived in Lexington (a neighboring town) and after talking with her, I felt certain Nathan was on the autism spectrum. My niece is on the spectrum and seven years older than Nathan, so I was learning to trust my gut and look at genetics as an indicator. Very scary.

I found out who the "experts" were in evaluating children on the spectrum and got our name on a list for an appointment that would not come until a year later, when Nathan was four.

In the meantime, he was delayed in speech, crawling, walking, etc. I put Nathan in Catherine's pre-school (different room) so he could learn to socialize and interact with other children -- a skill I wasn't seeing him display. Shortly afterward, the teachers at the pre-school strongly suggested removing him from that school setting (where he wanted to do nothing but swing all day) to be evaluated.

We agreed to accept their help to work with Nathan to learn play skills and social skills. Part of watching our son with these teachers was excruciatingly difficult. He would become upset, throw things and bang his head against the wall. It was exhausting and horrible to watch your child experience so much frustration.

Nathan was delayed at every stop. He never really crawled -- maybe some butt crawling. One day, however, when he was 18 months old, He got up and walked -- very slowly and deliberately. We were stunned. He didn't say Mama or Dada. How could this be? His first word came at nearly 4 years old, when I asked him what his favorite food was. He paused, which I was expecting, and then he came out with "Chinese," in a low deep voice. I'm sure he said Chinese because of all the talk we were doing around first Catherine, then Savanah's adoption. I almost died. His second word was "Catherine."

That's how our journey began to uncover what was behind the cherub-looking face of our son, who also was clearly challenged in other ways.

We sent Nathan to a large variety of schools, hoping educators could help him learn to manage his challenges (receptive language, sensory integration issues, etc.) -- none of which we had labels for at the time. Fortunately, Matthew and I paid for an evaluation, which would hold merit with the town's school system. We then hired an attorney who was known to help parents of children with special needs. He was able to help get Nathan the services he required from the schools in the town that we paid our taxes.

After about three years in early intervention special education programs in and around Concord, the school thought Nathan was ready for kindergarten in Concord Public School District. I was hesitant, but Matthew was hopeful.

Soon afterward, Nathan grabbed a girl by her poncho and dragged her around in a circle. Minutes later, school officials informed us that we needed to pick him up. Suddenly, the school was on-board to choose another educational alternative for Nathan. We began our search and were met with mixed success and failure, as I'm sure most parents of children with special needs find. There is no ideal setting or program for each of these children with their unique quirks and requirements.

Today, after many trials and errors at a variety of schools with a host of specialists, social skill classes, behaviorists (in and out of the classroom), etc., I realize Nathan survived so much. Now, he's a ninth-grader at a great school about which we learned. Many of his verbal expressions are that of a wiser, more mature person than his age. He works diligently at everything he achieves. Things don't particularly come easy to him except for the true interests that he has in collecting coins (he frequently uses the uncommon term "numismatics" for his coin collecting), understanding sports statistics, and the love he has for our dog, Cooper. He enjoys excessively grooming, walking and bathing Cooper.

I've told him I'm writing The Book of Nathan -- a collection of Nathan's sayings, such as:

"Hey mom, do you want to put on some romantic music, light a fire and talk about our relationship?"

Or, after watching television and seeing a commercial for Cymbalta (an antidepressant medication), he seriously said, *"You know Mom, depression DOES hurt."*

He also asked me, *"Mom, is it illegal to go to day college and still live with you?"* I want to say, tongue-in-cheek, but don't, *"Yes, it is Nathan -- we'll all be arrested."*

It's also amazing to see the boundaries that he can establish. For example, a friend of mine comes over with her two children, one of whom is obsessed with video games (in part because he doesn't have them at his house) and he is relentless with asking Savanah to play with him. Nathan simply says, *"Savanah, if you don't want to play the Wii, that's your right. You don't have to. Donny will have to understand."*

Nathan sees things as black or white. I often remind him that it's not good or bad, it just is. On the other hand, he'll ask me, when it's clear to both of us that he can't find where the mid-line is, *"So Mom, where's the gray area?"* He also loves to say he's stating "the facts," as he knows them. His concrete thought process is frustrating, to those close to Nathan, as he digs his heels in and it is difficult to persuade him that a different line is more accurate.

Nathan is affectionate, makes great eye contact and can mislead people who don't know him so well, since he appears to be age-appropriate. We, who are close to him, see differences when he interacts with others his age. He actually does better with younger children or adults, as they are more predictable. As his parent, I also see that he can be rude, dismissive and within seconds be the most loving and affectionate child on the planet.

My patience is tried daily as his mother, but I find him to be the greatest teacher of mine, as well.

All the while that I was growing accustomed to Nathan as an infant, we were proceeding slowly with our adoption of Savanah. Matthew and I visited Wide Horizons, our adoption agency, to pick up the photo of our newest arrival from China. She was a little doll. She had a tougher expression on her face than what we had seen with Catherine.

Savanah arrived in January 2000, a beautiful eight-month-old baby. We decided I would be the one to go to China, with my mother, to get Savanah. I had to be away from Catherine and Nathan for more than three weeks, had crazy jet lag and was frustrated and disappointed by Matthew's lack of preparedness when we arrived home.

Unlike Catherine's photo, with a baby blue background, Savanah was behind the typical red background used in all of the adoption photos I had seen, when taking photos of soon-to-be adopted babies in China. She wasn't smiling but she didn't look upset, either.

When my dad saw her picture, he began to call her "The Bif" because she looked like a toughie, in his mind. I was not amused by this nor was my mother, who I asked to join me on this trip.

Matthew and I thought it would be best for one of us to be with Catherine and Nathan. Looking back, I'm not sure I should have been the one to go to China but it turned out to be an experience of my lifetime with my mother by my side.

We did the typical long haul to China, via Seattle, and landed in Beijing, only to turn around a day later to fly to Wuhan, to meet our newest member of the family. The situation in China to adopt a baby is always surreal. Although I won't have that experience again in my lifetime -- it's an amazing process. We met the babies in Wuhan -- in the lobby of this massive hotel. I told my mom to go one way around the circle of caretakers and babies and I went around the other way, to find Savanah. All we had to go on was the little photo in a sea of babies. As I started to move towards my mother's side of the circle, I saw her -- Savanah Caitlyn Gao Chang Greenberg! My mother was talking to her and Savanah was reaching out to her with a big smile on her face -- as if she knew.

I started to shout out to my mom, *"That's our baby, Mom."* I put my hands out to this little China doll and, when she smiled back at me, I reached out to hold her in my arms. I melted. She looked like a mini-Olive Oil from the television cartoon *Popeye* -- her head was large, as compared to her little body. She had the most adorable pixie-cut hairdo. In contrast, Catherine had very little hair when we adopted her and it was matted down with a cradle cap. Savanah was nothing but smiles as we moved to a different level in the hotel to sign paperwork and feed her. She fell asleep in my arms. The heartbreaking scene came when older girls -- who were helping the caretakers with the babies and had most likely surpassed the age of adoption -- were holding on to some of the babies, not wanting them to leave.

My new friend, Brad (a dad on the trip, who was traveling alone to get their third child, Grace), asked for my help to get Grace. My mother brought over chocolates to give the girls and I asked if I could hold Grace. It was horrific to think about leaving the older girls to return to an orphanage and how they would miss these babies, to whom they had grown so attached.

While I was signing paperwork for Savanah, she was in the arms of a male orphanage director, toward whom she clearly had an attachment. For the remainder of the trip, Savanah held her arms out for every male we came in contact with, wanting them to hold her. I told Matthew that once we got home, she would have no problem bonding with him, as she had a "thing for men."

She was a dream baby -- just as Catherine was. She went to bed at 7 p.m. and woke up at 7 a.m. Savanah made a couple of "ah-he-he" sounds upon being put in her crib, but we shut the lights off and went to bed when she did (for the most part). I took sleeping pills to adjust to the time change in China, however, my mom was petrified that, if she did, she'd sleep through Savanah's crying and waking up. Never happened.

Savanah was eating everything I had brought to feed her and then some. She loved a pudding dish they served at breakfast and sometimes lunch. I could see her growing as we progressed during the trip.

My mom, who is not a lover of Chinese food in general and doesn't even like rice, bolstered her diet with Ziploc bags to grab the croissants they served at most of the breakfasts. Having been to China once before, I suggested we bring nuts, chocolate, peanut butter and crackers. However, that food was nearly gone just a few days into our three-week trip. Both Savanah and my mom were hungry. I, on the other hand, could, and do, eat almost anything and everything.

We met a Chinese family, who I came to know through a connection in Concord. Our architect, who we retained to re-configure our house, had suggested we meet a student of her husband in China while I was there. The student and his family were wonderful and so engaging. I think I gained 10 pounds while spending time with them at several restaurants throughout Wuhan with Savanah. My mom was often too tired to dine with us and her arthritis was killing her (from the cold and all of the walking during the trips we were taking each day). Each morning, we'd awaken by 7 and be waiting for a bus by 8 (that included time to eat, as well) to go somewhere in China to see the sights. We toured the Great Wall, temples, The Forbidden City -- all were amazing but tiring trips with a baby in tow.

Finally, the day came when we would take this little bundle of joy home and I could not have been happier. I was out of food for her, and Matthew and I were showing major signs of discontent with each other during my trip. The strain of distance, family obligations and lack of communication all contributed, I'm sure.

I also was craving time with Catherine and Nathan. My heart was breaking from being so far from them and I knew Catherine, especially, would be happy to meet her baby sister, and would have toys and other items ready to show and share with her.

By the time we left to go home, my mother was completely drained -- physically and emotionally. Between the grueling schedule, the joy and work of a new baby, living in a variety of hotels and sightseeing, it was clear that our hectic schedule had been just too much for her, especially by the time we boarded the airplane to go home.

I sat on the plane with another mother, Gabby, who had adopted Kylie, a baby who was in the same orphanage as Savanah. A rat or some other rodent had bitten Kylie. She had a bald spot on her scalp that Gabby was committed to helping her overcome, once we returned home. It was a long and exhausting trip. My mom and I tried to sleep and rest up before we had to transfer planes in Detroit, Mich.

We met a friend and colleague of mine, Lori, at the Detroit airport. She was one of my speakers, during my 600-store Staples speaking tour. She was lovely, brought balloons and visited with us before we had to meet our connecting flight back to Boston. Then, we were asked to collect our luggage. My mother was standing in a sea of suitcases and asked me where our luggage was -- as if I knew. I got a cart to throw our luggage upon and asked my mother to hold it still. I attempted to haul our luggage onto the cart, which kept moving backwards, along with my mother. I continued to request, "Mom, hold the cart, hold the cart!" That's something we laugh about today, but at the time it was exhausting and annoying. We made the shuttle bus to the connecting flight by seconds, which was a miracle.

Matthew, Catherine, Nathan, as well as Roberta and Jack (our nanny and her husband) met us at the airport in Boston. Their group also included friends and Matthew's parents, my dad, my brothers and their wives. A limo waited to drive us home. This was the first time Savanah had ever been in a car seat -- not good. Catherine had brought her new baby sister some toys to play with and wanted to sit next to her in the limo on the ride back from the airport.

Exasperated by Savanah's screams, Catherine said, *"I didn't know babies were so hard to make happy."* Poor thing.

Nathan seemed in shock, when it was obvious Savanah was a permanent family member. After sitting in our family room together for about an hour and Savanah would have nothing to do with anyone else, Nathan burst out in tears. This wasn't your picturesque homecoming.

However, Savanah adjusted well and soon after her arrival home she was content with people (other than myself) to spend time with her, feed her and hold her. It was a crazy busy time for all of us.

Roberta would leave our house feeling devastated that Savanah wouldn't want to go to her. I assured her that would change in mere days, and it did.

Savanah looked and acted like a little doll -- easy, like Catherine -- but seemingly happier all around. She always had a smile on her face and was far more mysterious than her siblings were. I miss that pure delight that she displayed as a toddler, now that she's a typical moody adolescent, like her brother and sister when they went through that stage.

I could say to her, as she crawled over to an electric outlet, *"No, no, that's hot, burn,"* and she'd be at it again the very second I turned my head. That was never the case with Catherine or Nathan. When you said, *"No, no,"* they walked away and didn't go near it again. Not this one.

It's funny when you look back at how you treated your first child -- if Catherine was having a nap time, we'd schedule everything around that nap. I was a little less diligent with Nathan, and sometimes there were days when both Catherine and Nathan were on opposite nap schedules. Therefore, we would have been in lockdown had I not started to break our nap rules. But, poor Savanah spent every waking and sleeping moment, it seemed, in the car seat with a bottle propped up as I was driving Nathan and Catherine to school, running errands, etc. It's sad for that third child and beyond -- or, maybe not. She seemed to adjust just fine and maybe, as parents, we screw up our first child (of which I am one) with the demands of self-imposed scheduling.

We had renovated our house and, meanwhile, moved into a temporary home for six months while contractors worked on it. Savanah adjusted beautifully to our new house, as did Nathan and Catherine. The stress of the move, renovation and massive expenses were getting the best of us, though. Nathan was also becoming more challenging as he got bigger and stronger and displayed real tantrums.

This house became an extension of me as I worked with a wonderful older woman who helped me pick paint colors, fixtures, appliances, and furnishings for a cohesive classic look. In the end, I felt like I had put much of my heart and soul into this structure and I became very attached to it. I was vested in making a wonderful home for my family to live in and experience.

Catherine was going through extreme problems with her skin, though, and Nathan was in the process of being officially diagnosed on the spectrum of autism. Savanah was just a baby and so much was going on at the same time -- the pressure was mounting and the distance between Matthew and I was obvious. Moving into a new welcoming surrounding I was sure would help. On the other hand, maybe not.

When we finally moved into our house after the six-month renovation, we were noticing water in the basement. One morning we called our builder, Josh, to come by and look. He showed up at 7 a.m. to investigate. Nathan and a naked Savanah came out to see what he was up to on our side porch. Josh asked them if they had turned the faucet on (that apparently went *into* the house for some odd reason). Nathan explained, *"We tried, and we tried, and we tried to turn it on, but it wouldn't."* Savanah whole-heartedly agreed, with an overwhelmingly big smile on her face.

Savanah was a trooper when it came to pre-school. I remember dropping her off at the Concord Children's Center with Roberta, Catherine and Nathan in tow, and talking to Savanah's new teachers. They were so kind and loving. I was thrilled about that, and they asked the typical questions you get when dropping off a two year old for pre-school.

"Has Savanah ever been in day care?"

"No."

"Has she ever been left in a pre-school-like setting before?"

"No, again."

"Okay, well, you know she's going to cry, but she'll be fine in a few minutes after that."

Okay, I thought.

I knelt down beside Savanah and I lifted her little face with its most precious little Asian features, (and her little turned-up nose) and said, *"Sweetie, Mommy is going to pick you up after you have some fun with your new friends and a snack with them, okay?"*

"Okay, Mama," Savanah replied.

We all blew kisses to her and said bye-bye, and she did the same in return with a big smile on her face. I closed the door of the nursery school and Roberta and I took one look at each other and started to cry. Savanah did not. She did amazingly well from that day forward. In hindsight, I think it was because she spent so much time in the back seat of the car, seeing me drop off Catherine and Nathan that she just knew I'd be back.

Savanah did like to get into things, though. At the age of six, just before I went to the hospital, Savanah had a screwdriver ready to push into an electrical socket. That's my girl. Always up for an adventure or experiment of some kind -- even if it turned out to be terribly dangerous. *"No, Savanah,"* I exclaimed. *"Come on, you're a big girl now and know that's dangerous."* She looked up at me with those beautiful brown eyes and I got the distinct feeling it would not be the last time I explained this to her. It wasn't.

When my brother Dick and his fiancée Liz lived with us, Liz made a habit of saving her spare change. Suddenly, it was missing and all eyes pointed to Savanah, who denied it for as long as she could. She always denied the obvious with a smile on her face, showing her guilt.

Finally, Liz kindly said, "*Savanah, I won't be mad at you, if you tell me the truth. Did you take my coins?*"

Savanah broke down in tears and showed her the pile of coins under her bed.

We were unable to find the numerous keys Savanah had removed from every antique piece of furniture we owned. I thought we would find them when we moved out of our house post-divorce, but they were nowhere to be found. No doubt, someone will dig them up in the back yard -- somewhere.

Later, for her eighth birthday, Savanah had an idea for her party.

"*Mom, I want to have a sleep over for my birthday.*"

I said, "*That's a great idea. Let's invite all of the girls in your class and pick a date.*" After experiencing Catherine's alienation in kindergarten of birthday parties and play dates, I was determined to never do the same to another child.

Savanah then said, "*Oh no mom, I want to invite only the boys in my class for a sleep over.*"

Terrific, I thought. As a marketing buff, I silently loved the idea. Identify your ideal target market (boys, in Savanah's case) and eliminate the competition in one fell swoop. Beautiful.

Savanah is a tomboy through and through. She has a huge heart and is one of the most thoughtful gift givers I've ever seen. She's a good friend, has a bit of a temper -- especially towards her deserving brother -- and loves my mother, who traveled with me to bring her home from China. She has her own unique sense of style and humor, and I just love her. She's also the tallest in the family, reaching 5'3" at age 13, surpassing her 17-year-old sister by inches, and is a lover of jeans and sweatshirts. She and Catherine engage in no fighting over clothes, etc. because they are true opposites, when it comes to appearance.

I'd missed the end of the school year due to my unexpected illness. Catherine had been on a field trip, when I got sick, so she'd been away with her class and came home to find her mother gone. Savanah had just turned age 6 before I temporarily vanished from her life, and I was sure she vividly remembered me puking in the parking lot of the karate place, where we had her birthday party. Nathan, my amazing, inquisitive miracle child, who asked more questions than a game show host, must have challenged everyone's patience while I wasn't around to run interference.

I was desperate to see them while I was recovering and made a special request that their father bring them to visit me. However, it was my brother and sister-in-law who helped me plan a visit, knowing how much it would help me to see them.

One of the nurses washed my hair the day before the visit. Since she wasn't going to be there the day the kids came, she told the weekend shift, *"I really want Nancy to look nice, when her kids come to see her. Make sure that she's wearing her nightgown, not the Johnny, and have someone come in that morning and wash her face and comb her hair."*

So often, it's the little things that mean so much -- especially when you're not feeling well. I wanted to cry. This woman understood how much seeing my kids meant to me and knew that I wanted to look as much like myself as possible, so they wouldn't be frightened. The fact that she verbalized what I couldn't say, thanks to the trach, was at the time, an overwhelming act of kindness.

Life Lesson #6:
*When someone instinctively "gets you,"
when you can't explain yourself,
that person is a keeper.*

As much as I anticipated the kids' visit, it was still extremely challenging on an emotional level. They were all feeling the effects of the separation. I'd worked hard to keep them from truly seeing how badly things between Matthew and I had deteriorated, but they're smart kids and they knew we were at odds. Now, I had the added worry about how they'd react to seeing me in such bad shape. The thought of scaring my own children brought on intense anxiety. I kept going over and over what I wanted to say to them -- if only I could speak.

Fortunately, the nurses were able to open up the trach a bit so that I could talk, at least a little. As much as I wanted to speak, though, it wasn't all pretty. Since I hadn't spoken in months, I had no control over my mouth. Those muscles were going to do whatever they damn well wanted.

True to form, the inquiring mind of my son wanted to know, *"Mom, why are there so many bubbles coming out of your mouth?"*

Great -- I finally get to see my kids and I'm foaming at the mouth. There's something they can file away to tell their therapists.

Catherine was brave and asked many questions. At age 9, she was very deep, and I could see her trying to take everything in and understand it as best she could. Matthew could barely make eye contact and kept covering his mouth and looking away. Was it disgust, guilt, empathy or horror?

Poor Savanah was in an absolute panic. My sister-in-law had tried to prepare her, but the machines, the noises -- hell, the sight of her mother looking like a science experiment -- were all just too much for her. I don't think my bald scarred head helped nor did the feeding tube in my nose. She couldn't even come into the room; she just stood out in the hall, shaking. It broke my heart to see how frightened she was and to know that there wasn't anything I could do to comfort her.

In retrospect, I guess that, perhaps, the kids saw me too soon. Savanah has yet to visit a hospital and won't even take a babysitting class offered by the local hospital. When she sees a hospital scene in a movie, she covers her eyes. Once, a woman with an oxygen tank came into a restaurant where we were eating. Savanah jumped into my lap and wanted to leave immediately. She was definitely the most affected by my illness, but in many ways she was probably the one least affected by the divorce -- most likely because she was so young.

And, here's where I must pause and share with you one of the wonderful things about writing a book. You have a chance to re-read what you have written and take back words that once said, can't be unspoken. This is precisely what I did. This entire chapter had originally been devoted to the dirty details of my divorce, but I decided to scratch the original chapter I had written about my ex-husband -- and I'm so glad I did.

My children will most likely read this book one day, as adults, and as a parent, my children and their needs come first. Period.

Life Lesson #7:

As children grow up, they should be allowed to come to their own conclusions about the imperfections and positive points of both their parents -- without the influence of the other parent's perception of their estranged spouse. So many divorced parents could benefit from those words. Maybe I should run an ad, erect a billboard?

Too often, I see men and women, decades post-divorce, lamenting the wrongs that were done to them by their former spouse. I know, I get it; it's difficult to let bygones be bygones. Love takes time, and getting over a love takes time, too -- but don't let it take decades. Your time and your life are too valuable, and getting on with being the new, single "you" needs your energy more than lamenting over what's done and can't be changed.

Life Lesson #8:

*Holding grudges hurts you,
more than it does the other party.*

Yes, there is a period of time when grieving the loss of a long-term relationship is imperative, and believe me, I did that. Unfortunately, for me, the timing was particularly lousy and I didn't get a chance to savor my little cry-fest. No, my pity party was one-upped by approaching liver failure, followed by waking from a coma months later, when I was slammed with two nasty truths: I was unbearably ill, and I felt absolutely hopeless. I, also, had to face the reality of not having my life partner with me, a truth that came to my conscious mind like a boulder rolling down a mountain -- with me waiting at the bottom to be crushed.

If a good marriage brings out the best in someone, a bad marriage can do the same. In the beginning, we really don't know the person we're marrying. I was age 24 and Matthew was age 27 -- we barely knew ourselves, let alone one another. I've heard it said that men marry women hoping they won't change and women marry men hoping they will change. It turns out that the opposite dynamic occurred in our marriage -- I didn't change (and perhaps he wanted me to), and he didn't change either (and I'm sure I wanted to 'tweak' him).

We went years without clearly understanding what the other wanted or what we expected from each other or our marriage. For instance, it was only when the marriage was over that Matthew told me he had always wanted me to be a stay-at-home, full-time mother. That was a role I could not imagine being, and I had made that clear at the onset of the relationship, but I understand that things change. Perhaps, what changed was Mathew's idea of what he wanted the mother of his children to do -- or not to do -- professionally. Too bad these conversations didn't take place as they came up in life.

Now, taking on that role of a stay-at-home mom is an amazing selfless act, and I applaud those who do it, but I know myself. If I am not happy, I will be no good for my kids. Giving up work that I loved was not going to make me happy. I know that mothering is a 24/7 commitment, whether you stay at home or work outside, but I needed to work in order to maintain my sense of self. I was stunned to learn, too late, that this had been so important to Matthew, yet, he never mentioned it. I don't think that would have changed my position, but at least we could have had a discussion and, perhaps, spared some anger down the road. I'm sure that expectations were not met on both sides.

Matthew is a great father and truly committed to our children. He continues to provide for them and spends equal time, to my time, with them now. This allows me to go on and live a more balanced life, and we are both much better able to spend quality time with our children, as a result. I feel fortunate that we don't have issues about visitation, especially for the kids' sake.

Would it be easier and more fun to feel victimized by the entire break-up and sing the "who done me wrong" song? Oh yeah, but really, only for a little while.

I opted to toss my original vent on what went so terribly wrong, during and in the aftermath of our marriage, because I just don't think and feel the same way about things anymore. Honestly, why bother?

This kind of insight, I believe, comes with age, maturity and experience -- most of which are missing when you marry in your 20s. Interestingly enough, though, my parents married young and each of my three brothers, who wed in their 20s, are all still happily married. Who knows what the winning formula is in a relationship? Clearly, I don't -- at least, not right now.

What I do know is that this book is about my journey: from the day my life, as I knew it, was yanked out from under me, to finding a new path of my reinvention. A road that has led me to where I am today: a successful business woman, a mother, and someone who has learned to take life by the horns and never take my health for granted. I now know what it means to be a survivor and that has made all the difference in who I am, as a person.

I'm grateful now that the separation and divorce, ultimately, came at my ex-husband's insistence. The choice wasn't left up to me. We had tried counseling, both individually and as a couple. But, all of that experience can be distilled into what I now see as a cold hard truth: It takes only one person to want out of a marriage, and no amount of couples counseling or individual therapy can pull you back together, when one party has made up their mind and isn't willing to give it another try. It's as simple as that.

I suppose we might have done what many men and women do in situations when the relationship has run its course: turned hostile or negative but stayed together nevertheless, "for the sake of the children." Or, continued to live our lives together -- but, separate -- denying both of us the fulfillment with a partner we both want and need.

While I'm sure that most children do want their parents to stay together, I believe they would prefer their parents to be happy flying solo rather than miserably married. Time will tell, and one of the perks of this memoir is that my children will have the opportunity to educate me on *their* perspectives as adults, when – and if -- they read this and see things from *my* perspective today.

I'm grateful, too, that I was only age 41 at the time of my divorce. Although having three small children isn't an ideal recipe for meeting and greeting potential suitors, being single in what I would consider my prime is not a bad thing.

We all know stories of women who are left behind when their husband of 35-plus years finds true love with someone 20 years her junior. She's left heartbroken and, in many cases, broke. Well, yes, that stinks but who says that her life is over? This may be the Aquarian in me but it's never been my belief that we are meant to be with only one love in our lifetime. I'm not big on the whole concept of soul mates and, although the notion is romanticized in our culture, reality plays out much differently.

Divorce rates are on the rise for first-time marriages, with diminishing returns for second- and third-timers, as well. It takes availability, timing, and chemistry (or sometimes none, initially) to forge forward with a relationship that's meaningful and, perhaps, lasting.

Life Lesson #9:

There are plenty of good men who will appreciate you for who you are, and you are free to go out and find them. Join a museum, take dance lessons, ask friends for assistance, go to book signings -- just get out there and give it a roll!

The fact is -- it simply is more difficult to find love, again, beyond a certain age, if you're not visible in your community or within your areas of interest. It's not impossible, but definitely more challenging. Instead of hiding under the covers and letting the world pass by, women need to get out there in order to meet appropriate matches. Honestly, more mature women, whose children are grown, have an advantage in this department. Make a pact with a friend, I know you have one, to live your life again -- solo or coupled. Both can be great.

My story of separation and divorce isn't unique -- half of you reading this book have undergone the same. No, what sets my story apart is the intensity of nearly losing my life and everything near and dear to me over a two-year period. My health, my home, my children, my ability to communicate through speaking or writing, my work, my desire to regain my independence and take care of myself -- and the list continues.

Divorce is enough of an obstacle in your life but facing death in the midst of all that, was excruciating. While lying still, helpless, hopeless and voiceless in that hospital, I experienced many days of internal debating, arguing with God, asking, "Why me?" What had I ever done to God -- or to anyone else -- to deserve this kind of physical, emotional and mental pain?

Maybe God didn't mind my questioning his path for me. He, eventually, allowed me to express myself, again, and by the time that would happen, I no longer felt the horrible, desperate, victimized feelings that had consumed me after I awoke from a two-month coma, in July of 2005.

Life Lesson #10:

It takes time to come to terms with some feelings. It's really true that, if you don't have anything nice to say, you shouldn't say anything at all.

I say all of this now with years of distance between the separation, my intense illness and slow recovery --

and ultimately -- our divorce. I'm not about "what ifs" and, though some moments are still painful and regrettable, every single thing I went through led me to where I am today. I now consider it all a gift. Nothing I would want to repeat or wish on someone else, but a gift none-the-less.

Now, getting from that hospital bed to this place of gratitude and acceptance took some doing on my part, and those who helped me -- from the doctors and nurses, to my family and friends.

CHAPTER 3

JUST BREATHE

How's this for irony? When I was young, I felt very comfortable in hospitals and medical facilities and thought about pursuing a career in that arena. I considered studying psychology or some other aspect of the medical field.

By the time I got to college, I'd fallen in love with television and broadcast journalism and my medical aspirations fell away. Imagine my surprise, when I wound up intimately involved with medical facilities anyway -- for all the wrong reasons.

It's hard to name one aspect of my time in the hospital as the absolute worst -- after all, there is such a plethora of fun stuff from which to choose. I had suffered severe organ failure and undergone two major surgeries, both rare operations that few people experience singly, let alone in tandem. I was comatose for two months and suffered terrifying hallucinations upon awakening. My bodily functions were completely beyond my control, an indignity that surpasses any I might previously have imagined. Moreover, I was terrified.

Looking back, I think that any of those factors on their own, and maybe even all together, would have been much more bearable but for one thing -- the trach.

Due to my dire condition at the time, the doctors had performed the trach, which has a hollow tube keeping it open, to allow me to breathe.

It is difficult to find words to describe the horror of having a trach tube, which I suppose, was medically necessary for me, but the damn thing literally took away my words, literally. All of them.

During my time in the Intensive Care Unit, there were so many questions I needed to ask, so many feelings I wanted to express. For a woman, who makes her living by talking, losing my voice was a nightmare. Until that happened, I had never realized just how valuable an instrument the voice is. Without it, a large part of me, simply, disappeared.

Without my voice, people behaved as though I wasn't even in the room. Doctors talked to my parents about my condition as I lay there, listening, unable to ask questions or offer any input. I am amazed my eyes weren't damaged by the amount of darting back and forth they did, as I frantically tried to get someone to notice me. One particular day, my doctor was explaining to my parents that the scarring on my brain looked, *"Good, healing nicely."* What? What scarring on my brain? I know I had a liver transplant but what the hell happened to my brain? This was before I realized I had half my head shaved, due to emergency brain surgery from the abscess that was found, after the hole was drilled in my head, prior to the liver transplant. No kidding.

Life Lesson #11:

*Just because someone can't speak,
doesn't mean they can't hear.*

I wanted to scream -- but I couldn't even whisper. I wanted to remind them all, *"Hey guys, I'm the guest of honor at this party! Can someone please ask me what I think about all this?"*

Sometimes, I just wanted to give my input on the little things, like what I watched on television. Right after I awoke from the coma, I found it difficult trying to pass the time when no one was with me. My mind was still awhirl with questions and fears, and my powers of concentration, certainly, weren't up to snuff. I liked watching talk shows on television, like Oprah and Dr. Phil -- shows that were entertaining without requiring too many mental gymnastics on my part.

One morning a doctor came into the room as I was watching the television show Regis and Kelly and said, *"Hey, why are you watching this? I read your book; you're much smarter than that! Let's put on CNN."* So, he changed the channel to coverage of Hurricane Katrina.

First of all, I was angry because the television seemed to be the only thing I had any control over, and he forced me to watch something I didn't want to see. Since I was still so heavily medicated, I found myself hallucinating that I was in New Orleans, in one of the hospitals where people couldn't get out in time. Fighting your way back from being comatose is not the time for anyone to judge your television viewing habits.

Aside from wanting to voice my objections, it was also frustrating to be unable to verbally thank the nurses, who were so kind to me. In addition to caring for my physical needs, some of them went the extra mile to help me feel a little more like a woman than simply a body in a bed. Margaret, my wonderful night nurse and savior from the feeble flutist, did my nails. She even shaved my legs and underarms. She seemed to understand the panic I felt, and taught me meditations that helped ease my anxiety. Those little acts of kindness were incredibly powerful, and I wanted to *say* thank you.

Life Lesson #12:

Never miss an opportunity to say "thank you."

What helped tremendously were the visits from some of my friends. My oldest childhood friend, Susan, who I've known forever and had been my maid-of-honor at my wedding, was there often. She and I are like sisters in many ways, bringing into our relationship all the good things *and* all the conflicts that come with siblings. I love her dearly and I've always felt that we'd known one another in a past life. I was, and still remain, extremely grateful that she made it a point to see me regularly, and for her efforts and time spent visiting me in the hospital and taking me out to lunch and to the movies, after I was released.

In addition, I truly looked forward to my friend Glenn's frequent visits, too. We are good enough friends that I didn't have to worry about not being able to talk -- Glenn knows me well enough without words. She helped me start to feel more normal, or at least as if normal wasn't a lifetime ago and would never come again. She kept bringing me scarves to cover my bald head, which was about the only thing that made me want to laugh, and want to scream, at the same time. I hated those damn scarves. However, more than anything, what she did was to give me something to think about other than the horrific ordeal I'd just been through -- something other than almost dying.

At one point, my deadpan humorous surgeon, Dr. Hanson, suggested, *"Nancy, you really need to do something with your hair."* At the time, I could only imagine what it might have looked like -- without the knowledge that half my head had been shaved due to the brain surgery.

I wanted my voice, I wanted a full head of hair, but what I wanted more than anything was to be with my kids again. Once I began to comprehend how long I'd been unconscious, I felt tremendous anxiety and sadness about not seeing my children.

How much I missed my kids was at the forefront of my mind, always, along with another harsh reality. Eventually, I'd have to be their mom again. I'd leave the hospital, go home, and need to take care of them. But, how on earth would I be able to do that?

That is when the prescription drugs tremendously influenced my life -- in a positive way. Let me tell you, there's just no substitute for the sweet relief of pharmaceuticals, when you're recovering from a total body shutdown and can't voice your fears.

It is funny, because when I first awoke from the coma I kept insisting, in my non-verbal way, that I was being over-medicated. What I didn't know was that I was being given super-high doses of medicine in order to keep me comfortable, and was gradually being weaned to lower doses. However, as the doses went down, my anxiety level went way up, and I started having major panic attacks. Enter my new best friend -- Ativan, a wonder drug that's prescribed for anxiety, of which I had plenty. Once I became aware of how much it was helping me, I actually started to request it.

At that point, everything threw me into a panic. I had to have regular liver biopsies to monitor the health of the new organ. My liver surgeon, Dr. Murray, was amazing. He could perform a biopsy in no time flat and cause me minimal discomfort. I trusted him implicitly. Sometimes, he even did the procedure right in my room.

Once, when I had to be taken to an Operating Room for the biopsy, I went into a full panic. This particular day, Dr. Murray was unavailable, and I was dealing with an intern who was charged with doing the procedure. I asked the intern through lip reading, "What the hell are you doing here? I thought Dr. Murray was going to do the biopsy." He attempted to explain that Dr. Murray had asked him to do it. I was none too pleased and let everyone know it by every non-verbal means I had at my disposal. As the long-term patient, who I was quickly becoming, I can't emphasize enough to the medical community how important consistency is in health care -- and in customer service, in general.

I mouthed to the nurse, "Can I please have some Ativan?" She agreed, offering to give me more just before the procedure. She even came with me and held my hand. I was so agitated, but her bedside manner calmed me down. That and the Ativan.

Life Lesson #13:

Never take for granted the women and men who devote their careers to caring for the sick. They are a marvel.

For every indignity that my body endured -- and there were many -- there was a nurse to take care of me and, more often than I care to recall, clean up the mess.

One man, who was about my age, worked the night shift. One night, right after he and Margaret had finished bathing me, I lost control of my bowels. There I lay, crying, humiliated, frustrated -- and mute. And this beautiful man said, *"Oh, Miss Nancy, don't cry. Oh, sweetie, you're making me so sad. Don't cry!"*

Ah, humiliation, my constant companion in the Intensive Care Unit. Know what's worse than having a rectal catheter? I guess the answer would be, not having one. That's the answer I think the nurses would give, anyway. The catheter, as disgusting as it was, kept things contained, or at least heading toward a designated receptacle, rather than all over my bed, my body. You know, right now I'm thinking I should buy each of the nurses a new car. How disgusting it must be to have to clean up human feces.

When I came out of the coma, there was way too much information to process that was more important than my bodily functions. I didn't think about the fact that, obviously, I'd been catheterized for two months. Once the catheter was removed, I kept having the sensation of needing to move my bowels, but I didn't yet have any control. It was not pretty.

Each day brought such a host of things for which to look forward. In an attempt to prevent bedsores and, hopefully, build up some muscle tone, I had to spend time every day sitting in a chair, rather than lying in bed. That would have been fine, if my body hadn't had the muscle tone of spaghetti. I couldn't even get out of bed without a nurse's assistance.

Nope, what I needed was that dreaded Hoyer lift to hoist me from my bed and deposit me on a chair, and then do it all again in reverse a couple of hours later. Whee!

I felt as though there was a never-ending parade of interns coming in my room to see the circus freak. Not realizing, at the time, just how rare my condition was, I couldn't understand why I had so much attention. I suppose it was better that I didn't know.

A few months later, when I had to return to the hospital for an endoscopy (a procedure using an instrument, called an endoscope, to examine the interior of a hollow organ or cavity of the body), Dr. Kelly announced I'd been the subject of the hospital's August 2005 mortality and morbidity conference. At the meeting, other physicians had asked him how he would treat another patient who presented with the same symptoms, and his response floored me. He had told them, *"I will never see another patient like this one in my lifetime. It just doesn't happen, what happened to her."*

I think I've mentioned this before, too -- I am nothing, if not an over-achiever. Yes, I'd have to say it was, definitely, better I did not know about that, just a month after waking up. Nevertheless, you sure do know you're having your share of bad days, when you're the subject of a mortality and morbidity conference.

Fortunately, though, better times were coming. Glory hallelujah, the day, finally, arrived when I would be taken off the trach. As much as I hated that damn tube, having it removed was absolutely terrifying. I kept feeling like I was suffocating as they weaned me off the respirator. I remember thinking, *"When I get out of here, if I ever do, I am going to suck in air all the time."* I just felt like I wasn't getting enough air. I kept trying to tell the nurses that there was something wrong with the machine, which made me feel like I was smothering.

They kept reassuring me -- or trying to -- that everything was fine. I heard a nurse say, "*Nancy, you're at 80 percent capacity,*" and later, "*You're at 84 percent; you're doing really well.*"

That might have been comforting, if I had any idea about what they were talking. The procedure hadn't been explained to me and I didn't know what to expect. All I knew was that I was in a constant struggle to get enough air into my lungs. I didn't know that I had to learn how to breathe on my own, again; I just felt like I was dying by suffocation. Lungs atrophy, just like every other muscle in the body. Who knew?

But I didn't die. Hell, no. I hadn't come that far to just stop breathing. I had work ahead of me, and I was determined to take a deep breath -- many glorious deep breaths. I would do anything, even feeling like I would die from a shortage of precious air, to survive and recover.

My mother kept trying to explain to me that I needed to go to rehabilitation -- something I was painfully aware of. She must have told me 13 times that she was going to look at Spaulding Rehab, known for its exceptional physical and occupational therapy. After her umpteenth explanation of where she was going I mouthed to her, "*I KNOW.*" Patience was wearing thin with me -- a potential sign I was actually getting better.

I was discharged from Beth Israel Hospital on August 4, 2005. Although I desperately wanted to go home and be with my children, that wasn't an option. First, I had no home in which to return, as Matthew had moved back into our marital home to live with the kids. Second, I simply was not strong enough to live on my own, let alone care for the children.

Off I went to Spaulding Rehabilitation Hospital, where I would learn to function, again. I was still getting sick from all the medications I had to take to prevent organ rejection. All this time, I was trying so hard to keep a strong face for my children and family.

I, desperately, wanted to reclaim what I once had, to get back my whole life. I knew I was starting from scratch. But, to be honest, I was so tired, and so scared of the uphill struggle that lay ahead of me.

At least now, when the trach came out, I could speak. Finally, I'd be able to voice my concerns.

Life Lesson #14:

Never take for granted the ability to ask for what you need and express your opinions.

I was determined that my experiences at Spaulding would be different from my time in the hospital. That was a nice dream. Let me tell you, rehab isn't all it's cracked up to be. Sure, I could talk, but that was about all I could do. My time at Spaulding was incredibly frustrating. I didn't know if I'd be able to do it all -- relearn every single thing I'd always done without thinking, like walking or grooming myself. The first time I stood up unassisted, I felt as if there was a thousand ton weight on my shoulders. Then, I fell while trying to use the commode, unable to support myself. To say that I felt out of control is an understatement; it was so hard to continue believing that I'd get it all back.

To make matters worse, at Spaulding I embarked on an eleven-week bout of intense nausea and vomiting that went on and on. There is nothing like attempting to learn to stand, walk, and button a blouse, when you're dry heaving throughout each therapy session. The nausea finally landed me back on Farr 10, the Transplant Unit at Beth Israel Hospital, for six weeks. I had dropped from 150 pounds down to 105, and was diagnosed with "failure to thrive." That episode was even worse than my initial hospitalization. After waking from the coma, although I felt awful, I had kept the hope that I would, eventually, recover and get my life back. This new diagnosis was a huge setback. "Failure to thrive" is, generally, a diagnosis given to infants, not adults. I knew I had to start my life over, but unlike an infant, I knew the obstacles that lay ahead -- and I had a lot more of them.

I was depressed; I was afraid. I felt that I would never get better and could not imagine what my life would be like. Would I ever again care for my children? What would happen to my business? Would I be dependent on my family forever? Would I ever go home?

Being placed in the Transplant Unit played a number on my head, as well. I was terrified that my body was rejecting the new liver. I was afraid that I was going to die.

But, no, dying was not in the cards for me.

In the end, an intern suspected I might have an inner ear imbalance that caused the nausea. Gotta love those interns! After she placed a Scopolamine patch behind my ear, I was eating within 24 hours. Food never tasted so good! I was sent back to Spaulding, once I was able to eat again, which did nothing to improve my mood. The good folks at Spaulding put me in the geriatric ward. Okay, I probably looked like I was age 100, but really?

Unlike Beth Israel, the rehab staff seemed overwhelmed and extremely short on time -- even to do the basics. I felt that they couldn't have cared less about me and resented having to do things for me. I even had to ask them for fresh bed linens, after three days of them remaining unchanged. This was a far cry from my time at Beth Israel, where it seemed like a constant and on-going process of keeping me clean and free of bedsores. I guess there were some perks that came with being the subject of the hospital's mortality and morbidity conference. During my three-month stay in the Intensive Care Unit, I had only one bedsore on the back of my head that, thankfully, was discovered when my hair was being washed one evening.

One of the hardest parts of rehab is seeing people who are in better shape than you are, and realizing how much work you must do to reach the milestone that they had. The only way not to let that feeling overwhelm you is to avoid looking at the big picture. I saw others who were in far worse shape than I was, as well.

Life Lesson #15:

Focus on how far you've come, not how far you still need to go.

One night, I hit my absolute low. I wanted to give up. I wanted to quit. I didn't have anything left inside with which to fight and just wanted to die. I was so scared and felt so alone. I couldn't even roll over to face the wall for privacy, so I just lay there and sobbed until there was nothing left inside me. Suicide was not an option (although it entered my mind more than I'd like to admit) when I thought about my children being left motherless.

When my parents visited the next day, my father asked me how I was feeling about what I was going through. He was the only person who had asked me that. I told him about falling apart the night before and about being afraid that I wouldn't get back to normal. He leaned down, looked into my eyes and said, *"Nancy, all you have to do is get better. That's all you need to think about. Just get better."*

I was, initially, none too pleased with his simplistic approach to healing and feeling better, but it started to sink in a couple of days later. I needed to adopt an attitude of gratitude for what little I could conjure up at that time. So, I began, and so did my recovery.

I felt like a weight was lifted from me. I swear I could even breathe easier. All that was expected from me was to relax and heal. I could do that. Western medicine got me through but I believe there was something more -- an inner strength and belief system that I didn't know was in me.

Life Lesson #16:

When all else fails, find something for which to be grateful. Start with baby steps and build from there.

In retrospect, I suppose my time at Spaulding was relatively short, considering all of the physical therapy I needed. After five weeks of torture, I was ready to go home. Now, all I needed was a place to go -- which I could call home.

CHAPTER 4

WHO SAYS YOU CAN'T GO HOME?

My parents still live in the house where I grew up, in rural Central Massachusetts. I don't mean Western Massachusetts, which has a real identity -- the Berkshires, made up of artists, spiritual and intellectual types who draw people from New York and New England. The Berkshires is known for its rural appeal and charm. It's where Norman Rockwell lived, for crying out loud. Tanglewood has beautiful music. It's far more preferable than Central Massachusetts -- if you ask me.

Barre, where my family lives, is still referred to, affectionately, with good reason, as "Barren." Trust me; the reference to it being "central" is an oxymoron.

There is nothing central about Barre. The nearest movie theatre or decent grocery store is more than 20 miles away. From about the age of 13, I counted the days until I could move on and out of my hometown, plotting my much-anticipated departure on the town calendar that I'd swiped from my parents. I *hated* growing up in Barre, and knew brighter horizons existed beyond its borders.

There was never any doubt in my mind that I'd go away to college. I couldn't see the point of, finally, getting out into the world beyond Barre's borders, only to return there every day. No, I wanted the opportunity to experience life fully and beyond my parents' door. Of late, some kids, willingly, return home to live with their parents after college. That's what my youngest brother, Paul, did. In fact, we thought he'd never leave. He'd probably still be living there, if it hadn't been for the encouragement from his girlfriend, Megan, who is his wife now. She wanted to live somewhere besides Barre. Things worked out just fine for him.

Other kids, like me, can't wait to leave for college and never look back.

Do you know the saying, *"If you want to make God laugh, tell Him your plans?"* Little did I know that I was offering God a real knee-slapper. Sure, college was the beginning of my adult life, but I'd eventually be returning home to roost, all right. The reason wouldn't be pretty.

There is no way, at age 41, to mentally prepare for returning to your childhood home and, once again, be living with your parents. No preparation -- believe me. I know because I did it, but not through any choice of my own.

Following my one-in-a-million combination of needing a liver transplant and brain surgery, spending two months in a coma and several weeks in rehabilitation, I was sure that I wasn't ready to live by myself. So, Barren, here I come.

As much as I knew that I wouldn't be able to live alone, my friend Glenn was pushing for me to find a place of my own, once I was finished at Beth Israel and Spaulding Rehabilitation. I don't know what she was thinking. I had no control of my bodily functions and couldn't talk or stand, let alone walk steadily or navigate stairs. However, Glenn's intentions were all good, if unrealistic. She knew that I would consider returning to my parents' home a huge step backward and had high hopes I'd be able to live independently -- if not right away, eventually. Her faith in me was encouraging, albeit unreasonable.

My dream, on the other hand -- not that anyone asked me what I wanted -- was to return home to my fabulous house in the 'burbs, to be with my children, get some live-in help and regain my strength. Good luck with that, Nancy.

The unfortunate reality, as I mentioned previously, was that my ex-husband had already moved back into our house and gained physical custody of our children, due to my obvious inability to care for them the way I once had. My new reality was a painful one that was forcing me to find a way station between near-death and recovery. It became blatantly obvious that I had to return to my parents' home, to rural Barre. I would be far from my children, friends and the community that had been part of my life for the past 20 years. There was simply no way that I could have taken care of my kids and myself. In truth, my post-surgical appearance and constant vomiting, prolonged fatigue and weakness, probably would have freaked them out.

After I had awakened from my coma, almost every day my dutiful parents made the 55-mile journey to Boston to visit me. I'd never felt more helpless, more frightened, than I did in the Intensive Care Unit; seeing my mom and dad -- their familiar and caring faces -- was the only comfort I had. I couldn't communicate with them, since I still had a trach and was unable to speak at the time -- and surely, I wasn't much to look at, as far as my appearance went. Yet, they came. To this day, when my mother drives me crazy, I remember that she selflessly overcame her panic attacks about driving on highways in order to see me, if Dad wasn't able to go with her.

Life Lesson #17:

Don't take for granted the lengths to which parents will go for their children.

Nevertheless, I still didn't want to have to live with them. Oh, I know that sounds awful. These dear people had endured so much agony, and now their ungrateful brat wanted to deny them the opportunity to have her with them all the time. Having said this, I am also incredibly grateful to them for putting me up, and putting up with me, during such a trying time. I had every meal cooked for me, was able to rest and recover and even see my children on weekends, thanks to my loving parents.

There's really more to it, though. As much as I didn't want to live with them, I also felt incredibly guilty about continuing to burden them with my overwhelming needs. They were already exhausted with worry and the daily drive to Boston. Did they really need to feel responsible for my constant care? They didn't deserve that and, quite frankly, neither did I.

Finally, after more than five months in the hospital and rehab, I was released into a waking nightmare, with a pick line in my left arm, a feeding tube in my nose and an unbelievable cocktail (I wish of alcohol) of I.V. drugs and other medications to ward off an organ rejection.

What's more, the I.V. meds had to be mixed every day. I had my own special recipe for the medication cocktail. My poor mother's anxiety attacks made her extremely worried about mixing the medicines, and I, also, felt uneasy about mixing them myself. I couldn't stop vomiting for 11 weeks straight and didn't have the strength or the clear head to even handle the bottles.

My brother Tim Jr. and his wife suggested I move in with them, their three teenage daughters, two dogs and a cat, which didn't sound like a very restful setting for convalescence. Their home is in New Braintree, Mass. -- perhaps an even more rural location than Barre. However, it was close to my parents' home and Tim Jr. thought it would give my mother a reprieve, while reducing her worry about mixing up my meds. He and my sister-in-law were both taught how to blend the drugs and deliver them through the I.V. As for me, I continued to be sick to my stomach -- literally.

My other brother, Dick, and his wife, Liz (who is a nurse, thank God), also offered to help. They lived in Fitchburg, about half the distance between Barre and my home in Concord. They, eventually, took charge of ordering and doling out the meds, which was quickly becoming a part-time job.

With all the sibling rivalry among my brothers and me when we were growing up, I would never have imagined how quickly and strongly they would rise to the occasion -- on so many occasions -- in the midst of such chaos. They are amazing men, who will never know the depth of my love and gratitude to them.

Life Lesson #18:

In the end, it's all about family.

My family felt that I'd be happier in Fitchburg because I would see more people from Concord and my social network than I would in Barre. The truth was, though, after I left the hospital and death's door, other people's lives moved on, too. For the most part, that's why many of my would-be visitors didn't show up for me. This realization gave me pause. It's reminiscent of what occurs after the death of a loved one. People gather around in the midst of the chaos but gradually fade away as time passes, resuming their own lives. I had to learn to do the same, in regard to those people who were no-shows during my illness, as painful as that was. Honestly, it did hurt for a couple of reasons. I was lonesome for my friends, for conversation and laughter. I was too sick to be a bon vivant, but I could've mustered a smile. I was depressed and scared, having no idea of what lay ahead for my kids and me -- and I had endless days to brood about that. Plus, I was kind of envious of people who still got to dress themselves, leave the house under their own power, go to work and use their minds. This was going to be a long, hard adjustment.

As it turned out, I didn't spend all of my time in one house. From one week to the next, I was never quite sure where I'd be staying. I might be staying with Dick and Liz; other days or weeks, my parents would encourage me to stay with them. Was it my effervescent companionship they all craved?

All of the moving around was exhausting. With the I.V. and other assorted paraphernalia, not to mention the constant vomiting and utter lack of energy, I dreaded each ride. Gorgeous New England autumn foliage flew by the car windows unnoticed, as my entire focus was on trying not to throw up.

Each trip to my parents' house reawakened my seventh-grade nightmares. I was staying in what was once my bedroom, now equipped with a bunk bed, television and a desk with a computer, on which my mother loved to play on-line poker. In order to set up the I.V., we had to Jerry-rig a host of extension cords that snaked from my room into the kitchen -- the only room in the house that met electrical codes, thanks to a remodeling project nearly 20 years earlier.

Envisioning a conflagration begun by old and faulty wiring, I suggested calling an electrician. While we, certainly, had enough to handle without worrying about starting an electrical fire, that call was never made. I was living out my worst nightmare in my childhood bedroom, fearful of dying in a house fire -- *after* having survived a liver transplant and brain surgery.

I should mention that my fear wasn't necessarily unfounded, because fire is not unknown to my family. My father affectionately calls my Nonna, my Italian grandmother, "Torch" and my mom "Flame" because they are smokers. A few years earlier, my mother's car had combusted in the driveway in the middle of the night. During one eventful trip to New Hampshire, Nonna inadvertently left a lit cigarette in the back seat of my dad's new car. Fortunately, the car was left mostly unscathed. However, with this history, I don't think it's any wonder that I worried about the house going up in flames. Having nothing but time on my hands, and with no strength to do anything else, I settled into a routine of observing my parents. When you're a kid, I guess you don't think one way or another about the things your family does. It is just who they are. Nevertheless, once you've had your own life, it's nearly impossible not to cast a critical eye on the people who raised you. Come on, you know what I'm talking about.

To this day, I don't understand my mother and father's relationship, although they are extremely happy and in love. So who am I to judge? Obviously, that hasn't been my lot in life.

My parents are complete opposites. My dad is anal-retentive and very particular in the way he does things, which is probably what made him a good accountant. He has a system for everything -- and I do mean everything -- and never changes his routines. Let me put it this way -- even as a diabetic, he drinks a beer right after his insulin shot. Why? Because that's the way he's always done it; it doesn't matter how absurd it is.

As for my mother, all I heard as a kid was, *"Your mother is a saint, an absolute saint."* Told, by everyone around you, that your mother is a saint leaves you a high standard against which to measure yourself. It also makes you wonder whether, if she's a saint, you might be the devil.

My mother, God love her, can be extremely naive. Sweet as she can be, she's not plugged into reality, sometimes. There is just no other way to say it. Once I drove home from college with my uncle, her brother, and arrived at the house high as a kite. I spent the afternoon laughing uncontrollably at my mom, and she never questioned my bloodshot eyes, odd behavior or extreme munchies. When I was still in high school, she once pulled an empty bottle of coffee brandy from under her car seat and said, *"How the heck did this get here?"* I couldn't believe I had forgotten to remove the evidence, or that it didn't even occur to my mother to be suspicious of me.

To be fair, maybe some of my mother's naiveté is not her fault; maybe, it is more of a defense mechanism against life's cruelties. In addition to taking care of us, she was extremely involved with her family, which was somewhat dysfunctional. Her older sister had mental problems that, at the time, unfortunately went undiagnosed. When my mom was age 21, her brother left a newly pregnant wife behind, when he was walking back to his Marine base in North Carolina and was killed by a drunk driver. Nearly 40 years later, my mother still bears the scars left by that devastating loss. She also has two other brothers about a decade younger than she is. Interestingly, my mother had my younger brothers, when I was ages 13 and 15. I think, maybe, raising small children, again, after she had pretty much been done with having babies so many years before, just added to her preoccupation.

Don't get me wrong; I truly love my parents. However, I had to wonder whether taking care of me was really in any of our best interests. All things considered, they did some amazing things for me during my recovery; at the top of the list was meeting Matthew nearly every weekend at a halfway point to pick up my kids and bring them to see me in Barre. For someone who is never at a loss for words, I can't even begin to express how much that meant to me -- and still does.

During those long months with my parents, I could barely look forward to life from one day to the next. Simply existing seemed to take every bit of my strength. Nevertheless, knowing that my babies would be with me for a couple of days did more to get me through each week than any medication.

Seeing my children also took the edge off all the frustrations I felt about everything, from constantly feeling nauseous, to being confined to the house. Close quarters can get very tight, especially when you don't have the option of leaving, for even a brief breath of fresh air.

Throughout my recovery, I had to return to Beth Israel for a number of tests and treatments, and my parents made the trip with me, every single time. God bless them. As if a new liver wasn't enough on its own, I also had to worry about infectious diseases because of my compromised immune system, which meant visits to dermatologists, neurologists and thoracic surgeons, to name a few.

The ride into Boston was always difficult for me, but that was the least of it. Once we would arrive, it apparently never occurred to my father to drop off my mother and me -- along with my I.V. and feeding tube -- at the hospital entrance. No, he would park the car, and then, we would all trek to the building together, at my agonizingly slow pace -- in winter in Boston. Do you think he thought the exercise would be good for me?

This type of behavior is actually typical of my father. He is a wonderful man, but how can I say this, he is somewhat oblivious to being a gentleman. He doesn't really get the concept of "ladies first," which is unusual for someone of his generation. It is probably the result of having been doted on by his parents, because he was diagnosed with diabetes at age 13.

My dad has always made a point of never being late for anything -- he never is. He held tight to his timely principles, even when it came to taking me to medical appointments, with the professional community that is probably more notorious than any other for keeping people waiting. Nevertheless, my dad would insist that we leave a minimum of 30 minutes earlier than necessary for each appointment, despite the fact that every single one ran late. Moreover, each time he would be in a state of shock and frustration when I wouldn't be seen for at least an hour after my scheduled appointment.

Yet, we still left 30 minutes early for the next appointment, when we'd settle in at the hospital and wait for whichever procedure. The fun just kept on rolling. I would be sitting in a hospital gown, waiting to be taken into the Emergency Room, and my dad would start asking questions.

"Why do you have to have this procedure?"

"Because the doctors found a spot on my lung and have to look at it."

"What do you think they'll find?"

"Jimmy Hoffa -- how should I know?"

"How long will this take? Should Mom and I go out to lunch?"

Honestly, I thought he and Mom were already out-to-lunch. Asking me questions that I couldn't possibly answer, drove me nuts.

However, I've got to admit that there were some pretty amusing incidents, as well. Six months after the transplant, I was hospitalized for 11 days due to a rejection episode and was prescribed steroids to try to save the liver. That's not the amusing part. A side effect of the medication is developing diabetes. Is this getting funny, yet?

Because of my dad's diabetes, I was already familiar with the treatment for the disease and how to test myself. On our way home from one of my appointments in Boston, we stopped for lunch at a McDonald's, which is -- I'm not kidding -- my parents' favorite restaurant. While my mother went in to buy food, my father and I sat in the car, testing our blood -- and then injecting ourselves with insulin.

There we were, shooting up in a strip mall, in a not-so-great neighborhood, in Cambridge. I mean, housing projects surrounded us. We must have looked like father-daughter drug addicts.

It is amazing, how respect for the absurd, can help get you through even the worst times.

With all of the moving around from house to house, not to mention the exhaustion and nausea that had become my constant companions, the holiday season really seemed to sneak up on me very suddenly. I was so grateful to be alive to celebrate another holiday, but hadn't given a thought to planning and preparing, because I simply couldn't do any of it.

What hurt the most was not being able to do the fun holiday stuff with my kids. This was supposed to be the most wonderful time of the year, but I sure wasn't feeling any of it. I think my greatest Christmas wish that year was to spend a day without puking, especially since the vile vomiting had already played such a prominent role in our holiday season, thus far.

On Thanksgiving, we had all gone to my cousin's home for dinner and I'd been especially excited since it was to be the first time that Savanah would be with us. I began the day with great anticipation. I couldn't wait to get there and have all of my children with me for the day.

Not long after we arrived, Nathan began to look a little green, and shortly thereafter, the poor boy was heaving his guts out. Apparently, he had picked up a stomach flu, and the vomiting just wouldn't stop. So much for a nice day with the family -- we had to leave early and go back to my brother Dick's house, where I was staying that week.

As soon as we got back, I put Nathan to bed, where he kept moaning, *"I'm dying! I'm dying!"* Naturally, I reassured him that he, definitely, was not about to die. Undeterred, and in full drama mode, he insisted, *"I'm dying! Tell me I'm dying!"* When I, finally, relented and assured him that clearly he was about to expire, he yelled, *"Keep me alive! Keep me alive!"*

I had been the victim of non-stop nausea for months, and now I was taking care of Nathan, while he threw up. I have to hand it to him, though -- it's not everyone who can make puking funny.

As Christmas approached, and my own nausea was making part of me feel a bit Grinch-like, I did want to buy gifts for the people I love. But, with my family already doing so much, there was just no way I was about to give them a shopping list, too. Somehow, I mustered the strength to point and click on a computer. To keep things simple, I ordered everything through Amazon.

Great idea, right? It is, certainly, logical and people with a lot more energy than I had were doing it. However, my Dad, the Certified Public Accountant, could not grasp this concept. He had volunteered his accounting experience to act as my personal financial manager. In theory, this may have been a good idea; in practice, however, not so much.

As most people probably know, Amazon does not charge for an item until it is ready to ship. This makes perfect sense to me. Not to Tim Stevens, my dad. As he went through my receipts, he could not comprehend how an order that totaled $437.93 showed up as only $103.45 on my bank statement. Try though I may, I simply wasn't able to explain Amazon's billing process. Sticking a pen in my eye several times might have been less annoying.

Did I mention that I had been heaving for 11 weeks straight and losing weight at an alarming rate? Attempting to explain the inner workings of Amazon wasn't doing a thing to help my recovery.

My mind kept drifting to a distant time, when I would have had a drink and just made the best of it. Now, however, the only cocktail I was imbibing was my lovely I.V. concoction, which, definitely, did not have the same effect on the situation that a Cosmo or margarita would have.

Not that there wasn't alcohol around for the taking, if I'd been able to drink it. My dad loves his Sam Adams Oktoberfest beer. Feeling quite the connoisseur of the stuff, he did what I suppose any beer-loving guy would do -- stacked cases of it in his home office, next to his desk.

Now, this would have been fine, except that he'd had arterial surgery on his neck, after which his local town doctor was going to -- wait for it -- make a house call. My father, certainly, did not want the good doctor seeing his huge stash of beer during that visit.

Did I say "house call?" Had we just reverted to the 1960s?

Not quite. I came to realize that the reason for the house call was really for my folks to show off their prize trick pony -- me! Surely, no young General Practitioner from Barre had ever seen the likes of me. It was fame by association, at the expense of the pony.

Fearing admonishment from his doctor, my father actually asked my mom to help him carry the cases of beer down to the basement, to get them out of sight. She refused, which ended up being a good thing, because the minute the doctor got to the house, my dad offered him a beer -- as we all suspected he would. You don't come to my family's home without being offered an alcoholic beverage, regardless of the time of day. Last year, my mom called me at 9:30 a.m. on Easter Sunday to ask if I'd bought beer for the dinner I was hosting. Do I know my family or what -- of course, I had beer!

If I haven't yet made it clear, my dad really does have some unique ways. This is the man, who taught me how to drive at age 16 by doing figure 8s -- *in reverse* -- to "get a feel for the wheel." My Uncle Mick, a driving instructor, was astounded at this ludicrous teaching method.

Obviously, I don't really get my father's logic, not having the analytical type of mind that he has. Yet, for someone so methodical, he sure spends a lot of time creating more work for himself. When he had nothing to do, my father would call Nonna and ask if she needed anything from the store. Had it been me, I would have gone to the store, bought what she needed, delivered it to her, gotten her money, and gone home. But, I'm not the logical one.

Nope. My dad is the logical one. He'd go to my Nonna's, get her shopping list and money, drive around town to different stores in no efficient manner, deliver her purchases and head home. Half the time, she would call the house to say that she had forgotten to mention an item or two. Of course, my dad didn't have a cell phone, so when he came home I'd deliver the message and out he'd go back out to pick up the rest of her things.

Life Lesson #19:

Honestly, I truly admire my parents' relationship with my Nonna. They do a lot for her and enjoy her company. Remember this when Mom and Dad are her age, and remember not to complain about
helping them out.

Personally, I think my father just really liked to drive. It's about the only way I can explain my parents' regular journey from Barre to Rindge, New Hampshire -- to buy groceries.

Why would anyone drive for more than an hour for groceries? I guess the reason makes sense to a Certified Public Accountant -- there's no tax in New Hampshire, so cigarettes and beer are much cheaper there. However, wouldn't a Certified Public Accountant also realize that it's not worth spending nearly $4 per gallon for gas, in order to purchase less expensive beer and smokes? Apparently, however, the more expensive trip made some kind of sense to him.

On a freezing January day, my parents insisted I join them and my Nonna on a grocery jaunt to New Hampshire.

I can only hope that they believed the outing would have some rejuvenating effect on me, because it's impossible to comprehend that they didn't realize I was in no condition to take an hour-long joyride, let alone be seen in public. There was a feeding tube hanging out of my nose; I was wearing a wig to cover the brain surgery scars; and I was not a pretty picture -- certainly, not ready for prime time.

To add to the lovely effect, I was suffering from an accelerated form of osteoporosis and bone degeneration that made it extremely difficult to maneuver myself in and out of cars, beds, sofas, or anything that required rising from a sitting position. So, I also was a hunchback. Moreover, I was about to become a star. My doctors had told me that, thanks to my amazing bone condition -- which they initially thought I had dreamed up -- they wrote a piece for The New England Journal of Medicine. Ah, the lengths some people will go to for fame.

After enduring the hellish ride to the supermarket, I did put my foot down and told my parents that I was not up to perusing the aisles. Really, after months in the hospital and rehab, the supermarket was far from what I'd envisioned, as my debut outing. Instead, I decided to sit at the front of the store at the end of the cashier stations and wait for them to finish shopping. Despite my reluctance to parade myself up and down the aisles, I did put in an order for *fresh produce* --

hummus, bleu cheese and all the "exotic" foods I craved that weren't on my parents' grocery list.

I've got to say that maybe my parents were right about my needing this trip -- if not for the reasons they thought. For the first time in months, I found myself looking at, and thinking about, people other than myself. I was amused.

You know what it's like to sit in an airport and people-watch? Well, I didn't have any airports in my immediate future, but that market was the next best thing. It's kind of incredible to consider how many people, apparently, *don't* consider their appearance before they leave the house. Do they even look in the mirror? Maybe they do, and really think they look good. Either way, some people's attire was damn scary.

As person after person went through that checkout line, I was repeatedly amazed and amused at what, apparently, passes for acceptable fashion in Rindge. A woman walked in at 3:23 in the afternoon wearing a floral flannel nightgown under a parka, with three kids under the age of 5 in tow. On my worst day -- and believe me, I've had plenty -- I would have figured out Plan B for dinner, rather than show up at a grocery store, at almost dinner time, in my pajamas!

To be fair, I suppose that I presented my share of entertainment value, as well. I'm pretty sure it's not every day that the good people of Rindge got to see a post-surgical marvel like me at the grocery store. Although, honestly, I don't recall feeling as if I were on display. Hmmm...maybe I fit right in. Could Rindge be the place where I belonged? The very thought made me shiver.

As I waited for my parents and Nonna to finish shopping, I couldn't help but remember the one-woman show written and performed by Julia Sweeney, who played Pat on *Saturday Night Live*. She, hilariously, described her parents moving into her home to care for her during her bout with cancer. Now, that was a better deal than mine, I realized. *They moved in with her* -- not the other way around. At least, she was in her own home and not exposed to the extreme and unusual torture of being a middle-aged person living in her parents' house.

One of the funniest parts of Sweeney's play is about her parents' amazement at the fact that she'd spent $8 on a jar of marinara sauce, as if it were some rare food available only to members of the royal family. She wasn't a queen, after all!

I could picture my mom and dad shaking their heads over the frivolity of paying $10 for bleu cheese, as they picked up the items on my list. I knew they'd be grumbling about how their daughter could have developed such exotic taste. Nevertheless, this was my food palate. This wasn't the palate of a person who had been raised on canned green beans and too much red meat! Nevertheless, it was mine.

I had to wonder whether my parents read the paper or listened to the news. Were they aware that red meat was unhealthy at every meal? My mom has always been a decent cook, although not a very creative one. I swear that she served stuffed peppers three times a week. To this day, I gag at the thought of them. When she found something that worked, she stayed with it. No experimenting for Kathleen and Tim -- salt, pepper and maybe some oregano was all you got in their cuisine. You won't find any cumin or cayenne in my mom's spice cabinet.

My parents' diets were appalling to me. I craved fresh food, fish, fruit, not the ever-present side of beef that appeared on the dinner table. I, desperately, wanted to overhaul my parents' eating habits, which I guess is another drawback of revisiting your childhood home at my age. I wanted to teach them everything I'd learned after I'd left their house, but I just didn't have the strength to argue about it.

After more than an hour, I finally saw Dad, Flame and Torch coming through the checkout line. Thank the good Lord. Ready to go! As we headed toward the door I told them, *"I have never been so happy to see such good looking, energetic and might I add, well-dressed people, as the three of you."*

I may not have had any marinara sauce, but, by God, I had some fresh produce. It gave me a glimmer of hope after a long trip and a very long day.

The truth is, that trip to the supermarket gave me plenty of time to reflect. I, finally, came to the conclusion that, basically, who did I think I was? My parents are happy. They're living the life they want to live; who was I to tell them it was wrong in any way?

They'd always been great parents, and after all they'd done for me, since I'd gotten sick, they now had my eternal gratitude for their kindnesses too numerous to count.

However, that still didn't mean I wanted to spend a whole lot more time in Barre. As much as I loved my mom and dad, I truly needed my children. Though my parents would surely continue to venture to New Hampshire for groceries, I decided to "Live Free." I, once again, began plotting my escape from Central Massachusetts, back to Concord -- the place I called home.

CHAPTER 5

THAT'S WHAT FRIENDS ARE FOR

It's so true -- people do come into your life for a reason, a season or a lifetime.

Back when I was still married to Matthew, I had a circle of friends that I socialized with all the time. My husband and I entertained often and I thought the people who surrounded us would remain my closest friends for a long, long time. We had a lot of fun, planned many parties, ate, drank, and shopped -- who wouldn't want to be us with our warm and lively circle of friends? We seemingly had it all.

Of course, it's easy to have, and to be, a good friend -- when the sailing is smooth. However, when the chips were down and the going got tough, with divorce proceedings and my illness making a shipwreck of what was once my life, some of those friends became scarce. There were some, a few, who stayed by my side through it all; I am eternally grateful to them for that.

But, for just this one moment, give me permission to vent, please. I simply could not believe how many friends just left me. Crises bring out the best and worst in people -- happy occasions can do the same. It's not easy to predict what someone's reaction will be in good times or in bad. Nevertheless, actions speak louder than words.

The horrifying thing about living out my worst nightmare is to have gotten more friendships, than I expected, so wrong on so many levels. At the time, probably because I was ill and vulnerable, parts of this friendship ordeal brought me to my emotional knees.

Some of my so-called "best" friends never even came to visit me in the hospital -- including my estranged husband. After 16 years of marriage, the one friend I never expected to lose, walked out of my life. In truth, perhaps, the only reason we lasted as long as we did was that we didn't spend all that much time together. Looking back at those times, I realize how deeply asleep I was -- how much I wasn't seeing about the day-to-day routine of my own life. I was blind and numb, ignoring all the signs around me that something wasn't quite right in my marriage -- and in some of my friendships.

This is what happens when you aren't living your own life any more. Not the life that you really wanted. Everything I had, and lost, wasn't real; not the way it should have been. Life changes happen quickly and abruptly sometimes, and it can be hard to find your footing, after a tornado blows through your life. But, things are so much clearer now that I know what is important to me. I know why, and for what, I am living my life. I know I am still here because I can pass along lessons learned to my children and to other people I now choose to make part of my life. The gift of surviving so many different challenges will teach a person those kinds of lessons.

Life Lesson #20:

Going through the range of feelings needed to heal, gets better, and you do get over them. It isn't easy, but in the end you are free to live life on your terms. Keep your friends close and always be there for each other. That is what will get you back to laughter at the end of the day.

Apparently, many of those with whom I had shared laughter and so many of the good times were unwilling to participate in the bad. People, already, had drifted during the end of the glory days of Nancy and Matthew. However, when I hit bottom, healthwise, many of those who had remained just disappeared -- going on with their own lives and probably just waiting to attend my wake and funeral. I wonder how many pondered which little black dress would be most appropriate for a dear friend's last hurrah. I sound a tad harsh, I'm sure. But, if the shoe were on the other foot, or the trach in another person's windpipe, or the baldness on the other head, I'm thinking they would feel much the same way.

Life Lesson #21:

When a close friend, relative or even an acquaintance is clinging to life in a coma in the hospital, spend a few minutes at their bedside whispering encouragement and praying for their recovery. If you can't see your way clear to do that, you can be sure you are one of those people who was in their life for a reason or a season, but certainly not a lifetime.

I don't deny that it hurt terribly, when some of the people I considered good friends disappeared at the time I needed them most. In retrospect, I am glad to have had them in my life, at some point. Even superficial friends, who I thought were real, served a purpose during the times they brought fun and laughter to my life.

Some of the people you meet are there for the duration, others run out on you as soon as the dance music stops. When I was at my lowest, I found out who was who, resulting in a massive shake down among many of the people I thought were closest to me. Maybe, I should have seen the writing on the wall sooner. There's nothing quite like experiencing multiple major life crises to put it all in perspective.

It took almost dying for me to discover two important things about friendship:

I had a few really good friends on whom I could always count.

In the end, that was all I needed.

Life Lesson #22:

Friends, and the friendships they offer, come in all shapes and sizes. Like the typical woman's wardrobe, some of them just no longer fit our body or our style and need to be cleared out from our closet. Hand them down, toss them out; either way, ending friendships that have run their course, though not easy, creates more space for those that continue to be a vital part of your life.

Everyone, woman or man, has that one special friend -- or should have. This special friend is the one who is always there to lift you up and slap you back into reality, if needed. This is the one who will wipe away your tears with one hand and give you the number to a fabulous attorney with the other. This one is right at your side while you make your stand to take back your dignity. They have your back, no matter what, and can always be counted on to offer a stab -- at your ex-husband's expense -- or fix you up with their husband's best friend, who recently lost his adored wife. They are the ones who can make you laugh, when what you really want to do is cry. You know this friend, you can come up with their name right now, and it brings a smile to your face.

Glenn and I first met at Water World in New Hampshire, an unintentional, unwitting gift from Matthew. He and Glenn's husband owned businesses on the same street and had become friends through proximity. Matthew had invited him, Glenn and some of her family to his annual company summer outing at the water park.

Water parks conjure up two unsavory self-images for adult women -- or at least for most of the adult women that I know. Not-so-itsy-bitsy bodies stuffed into the least visually offensive bathing suit possible, and frizzed out hair that normally looks perfectly fine, except when exposed to humidity. Yeah, hot sun, bathing suit, humidity and frizzy hair. That's not really my idea of a pleasant afternoon outing. My husband knew quite well, by this point in our relationship, that I'm not a fun person at water parks, top sales fairs and all those things that he loves. I hate them.

When Glenn and I sat down on a bench together, the disdain that we both felt for the situation must have been written all over our faces. One look was all it took to know that we were in the same boat. We exchanged smirks and witty banter about hair and bathing suits, which opened the door for relaxed laughter between us. It was just so refreshing to have someone who really understood and was honest enough to talk about it.

While everyone else was aimlessly splashing and sliding down water slides, Glenn and I were wading into the beginning of a meaningful, beautiful friendship.

After that day, whenever I went into town to see Matthew, I stopped by to visit Glenn. I learned that she wanted to start her own business but wasn't sure where to begin. I, of course, jumped right in to do what I could to help her. That's what women do. That's what friends do. At the coffee shop around the corner, we discussed her plans, marketing ideas and all the other things she needed to do.

We fast became close friends and were very involved in each other's lives. We spent time together with our husbands, as couples, as well. We regularly had dinners at their house or ours. When things between Matthew and I began to go south, Glenn was right there. Actually, it was because of her openness that I knew the issues between him and me were even bigger than I'd thought.

During one of her phone calls, she told me how Matthew had unloaded on her about our marital problems when she had stopped by his shop one day. What he told her, and she shared with me, was really the beginning of the end of Matthew and me. I just didn't know that at the time.

I didn't know what to say to her, except, "Thank you for telling me." Glenn understood and told me to call her if I needed anything. I muttered that I would, but in truth, I just wanted to get off the phone. I was so embarrassed and in shock. Glenn was *my* friend and while I had kept mostly silent about the problems we were experiencing in our marriage, Matthew had chosen to voice his complaints about me to her.

Life Lesson #23:

When your spouse goes public, especially confiding in YOUR friends, it's a sign that things are in an unstoppable downhill spiral in your relationship.

The day that he moved out, Glenn came over to be with the kids and me. Hearing the front door open and her voice echoing greetings into the hall, saved my sanity. I was accustomed to being alone with the kids most of the time but knowing that Matthew wasn't going to be walking through the front door any longer was really hard.

Life Lesson #24:

Change is hard to do alone. Be open to the support and the company of friends and family.

Even harder was the fact that I needed to be up front with my children, who had no idea what was going on and deserved to know the truth.

With Glenn at my side, I sat down with my kids and took a deep breath. *"Guys, I have some news to tell you."*

My son, Nathan, was the first to speak, *"Is it bad news or good news?"*

I paused, looking at Glenn, *"Well, it's kind of sad news."* She nodded her head, letting me know that I answered that one right.

I hated what I was about to say. The last thing I have ever wanted to do is hurt my kids. I did the best I could to say what I had to tell them in honest and simple terms that they could understand.

"Well, the sad news is that Mommy and Daddy have decided that we can't get along, and it would be better if we lived separately right now. So, Daddy moved out. But, Daddy still loves you. I still love you. You're still going to see him, but he's not going to be living here anymore."

I held my breath, waiting for a response, but they were oddly quiet. Catherine simply asked for more pasta primavera, but then Nathan spoke up.

"But Mom, that means you'll have to learn how to play basketball."

"I'll do my best to learn how to play basketball, but you'll still have Dad to do that with you. There will be other things that Mommy will do with you, too."

To soften the blow, I told my children that we could send daddy a care package of things they think he might need in his new home. Savanah wanted to send him some gummy bears and sour patch kids. That was much more than he deserved in my mind, though I didn't say it aloud. I was really expecting more questions, tears and emotional reactions but not one tear fell. Not one.

I went to bed almost right after dinner that night; I was spent and had to make a court appearance in the morning. Glenn, my lifeline, stayed up with the kids, keeping them upbeat and distracted from dwelling on the major life changes that were to come, through no fault of theirs. Catherine and Savanah offered to give her a massage and covered the poor woman in lotion. She made Nathan pancakes the next morning, promising, and then forgetting, to top them with fruit. She did not even bat an eye when he let out a deep-voiced scream of, *"Hey, where's the fruit?"* She simply replied, *"Oh, I'm so sorry, let me make you some more."*

When she called the next night, as if on cue because I really needed her perspective, she asked how I was holding up. *"Ready for a glass of wine, yet?"*

I smiled into the phone. We loved our wine.

"Glenn, honestly, I can't thank you enough for last night and for everything these last few weeks."

Life Lesson #25:

How do you tell who your real friends are? That's the person who will actually drop everything, come over, feed you and your family, and put your kids to bed. That's the person who will be there to help break bad news to your kids, not just share in the happy and joyous moments. Sometimes, all you need is a good friend to talk with to get clarity about a situation; other times to pull you back from the edge.

"Glenn, I didn't know how I was going to tell the kids their dad left…"

"Come on, Nancy. What are friends for?"

Glenn might consider giving lessons on that subject because I'm not sure most people know the correct answer. It seemed that many of my so-called friends had developed the habit of not calling me back during those days and I could only imagine what people might be saying -- or gossiping -- about the breakup of my marriage.

"Nancy, I figured the kids were going to be very upset that daddy wasn't coming home. Honestly, I was worried for them, as well as for you. I think you and I both understood that the marriage was over. But I have to admit that they took it pretty well, actually."

What she had said about how the kids were managing was true enough, but as for me...

"I don't know, Glenn. Sometimes I think if what he wanted was for me to be waiting at the door with lemonade, maybe, I should have been able to do that for him. Maybe, I made a mistake."

"Okay, do you want me to slap you through the phone now or in person tomorrow?"

It was the comment and the laugh that I needed, and Glenn knew how to deliver. "You're right, it was just a moment of weakness; I would never be happy like that. I love being a businesswoman and a mom. I just need to find a way to make it all work without Matthew and the drama that surrounded us."

Glenn went on to point out that, at least, I had been wise enough to marry a man who could support me financially in divorce. Heaven knows, he hadn't supported me the way I needed in marriage.

"Nancy, you were instrumental in Matthew moving forward. He would not be as successful today had you not been a part of his yesterday."

Life Lesson #26:
Just because someone doesn't acknowledge your impact on their life, doesn't mean you didn't make one.

I know that I wouldn't have been as successful myself without the sent-from-heaven Roberta, who turned out to be so much more than my office assistant and nanny, and more like a mom to me in every way that matters. She and her husband, Jack, are family to us now, and have been the answer to many prayers. My kids refer to her as Nana Roberta, and the name is fitting.

They have seen us through sickness and health, through better and worse -- the very worst times I can ever imagine. They knew, before anyone, the trouble that was brewing in my version of Eden. Without them -- their love, loyalty and support -- I would never, again, have found the peace of mind that I temporarily had lost. Maybe, I never even had it at the beginning.

Glenn and Roberta, these two amazing people, exemplify the meaning of friendship. Through the years, I have formed a bond and a trust with them that went above and beyond the call of duty. Savanah, my youngest, wants to spend almost every weekend with Roberta and her husband, Jack. It's Jack who will be there after school, or the practice or lesson of the day, to drive my kids home if I'm detained. I count them among my dearest friends and count my blessings daily for having them in my life.

Life Lesson #27:
Be kind and pay attention to the people around you. The people you work for and the people who work for you, your position in life and your status in society do not dictate who is, or will be, your friend. Most people rarely have the benefit of seeing people for whom they really are -- an eye-opening experience to be sure.

One of many good things that, ultimately, came out of my divorce proceedings was a recommendation from the presiding judge, who had issued a restraining order against my husband after an "unfortunate" incident outside the courtroom. He suggested that I join a support group, Women with Controlling Partners. I hadn't a clue what to expect but I thought it would help to see that I wasn't the only one with problems, and, maybe, help me find some of the answers for which I was looking.

I never expected that I would meet some of my best friends there, while I was in the group. I never expected to have such a wave of changes happen to me. To this day, joining that group remains one of the most memorable bizarre times in my life. That's saying something. These women saved my life from sadness and loneliness and helped me find the hope that I had lost.

I hit it off almost immediately with Bethany, Nadine and Connie. We'd go out for coffee, after the group sessions, and talk about our personal situations. It was nice to get to do the girl thing, and be able to talk to people who understood what was happening in my life. We would commiserate with one another about how odd it was to end up with these men, who now seemed so different from when we first married them.

Life Lesson #28:

Nothing helps you conquer anger like laughter.
That is one of the ways we were all there for each other --
to bring a smile, when someone needed it most.
That is the true point of a support group.

As the lyrics to the song go:

Smile, though your heart is aching
Smile, even though it's breaking
When there are clouds in the sky, you'll get by
If you smile through your fear and sorrow
Smile, and maybe tomorrow
You'll see the sun come shining through for you

Light up your face with gladness
Hide every trace of sadness
Although a tear may be ever so near
That's the time you must keep on trying
Smile, what's the use of crying?
You'll find that life is still worthwhile
If you just smile

That's the time you must keep on trying
Smile, what's the use of crying?
You'll find that life is still worthwhile
If you just smile

I love that song and find it so ironic and interesting that Charlie Chaplin, one of the great comedians, wrote those lyrics.

We all had our own reasons for being in the group. Bethany was directed to join by her therapist. She was going through a divorce and needed to get support for herself, so she could be there for her kids. Her husband was a belittling pompous ass, who tried to make her feel like she was nothing. She stayed home, took care of him, the house and kids, but when she tried to do something for herself outside of the home, he wouldn't allow it. After a while, she knew their marriage would not work and she wanted a divorce. She needed the group to help in dealing with her passive-aggressive, controlling partner.

Nadine was in school and in the midst of a divorce, at the time we met. Her story made mine sound almost normal -- despite the fact that I had already undergone a major health crisis.

Her ex-husband was a sex addict, right down to hiring prostitutes, being blackmailed and publicly humiliated. She had married and divorced him twice and just wanted to be done with him. By the time we met, she was doing fabulously and in a great relationship with Neal. They both had children and lived together in a big, loving household. Interestingly enough, after meeting and dating for a while, Nadine couldn't believe she was expecting a baby with Neal, who had a vasectomy several years before. Baby Nicole, it turns out, was a true and unexpected blessing! She was also a reminder to be diligent about birth control.

We have gatherings at their place with our children, swimming and barbequing and enjoying our lives and our friendship together. Meeting Nadine was proof positive that I would be able to come out on the other side -- better, stronger, happier.

Now, Connie was the live entertainment. She is so Samantha, from the television show *Sex in the City*, a real man-eater, and men just loved her. She would be with someone new all the time, but seemed to have problems breaking up with them.

She, suddenly, started dating someone seriously, and though he does some things that irritate us as a group (like inviting himself along to our gatherings and being a bit flirty) she says it doesn't bother her. Everyone has a different idea of what is acceptable and a different threshold of tolerance, I suppose.

Support groups are not one-size-fits-all, but a single common bond can open the doors to new people, new insights and new beginnings. I highly recommend them. We were healing and getting our lives back. Our group was an anchor that kept us somewhat stable through the hectic changes of our lives. We have gone through so much togethe, and we have all grown. I not only found help, through some very tough times, I found true friends.

Life Lesson #29:
Differences contribute to the value of friendships, just as much as similarities.

With the help of the fabulous women in my support group, I recognized what I did not want in my life anymore. I identified the red flags as danger signals. Together we talked about it all -- the shame, the denial, the fears -- and found support and the courage to get over them and, finally, put them in the past.

Though I was a credible witness to losing the life I had known while I was going through my separation, it was interesting to learn, later, about the reactions of other people, during a time when I could not really bear witness or represent myself.

When I hit the depths of despair, health-wise, many of my friends acted oddly, while others -- some of them strangers -- reached out in the most unique and caring ways.

Though I would not have chosen to make true lifetime friends in this manner, I was not exactly given an option. Without some of the people I came to know, as a direct result of my illness, I don't think I would have survived, physically and, definitely, not emotionally.

Some amazing nurses cared for me throughout my illness and though we don't carry on a friendship, their nurturing and support were precisely what I needed, at the time. Margaret and Frederick were in my life for a season and a reason, and the small things they did made such a huge difference. Margaret would waltz in saying, *"Okay, we're going to give you a bath and then we're going to shave your legs and under your arms today. That's what we need to do."* Most people can't relate to the relief and elation I felt at being treated like a woman.

Then there was Frederick, the nicest Intensive Care Unit nurse you could possibly imagine. He had said that he could tell by my skin and teeth that I was a woman who took care of her body, and that my body would take care of me. He treated me like a lady, and I remember feeling like one, when he complimented me on my French toenails.

Life Lesson #30:

At any given moment, normal everyday things can become the most important thing you can do for a person, and make for the most touching of memories.

Of course, my childhood friend Susan was there for me throughout the duration of my illness and recovery. Susan bought me a great Raquel-Welch-style wig, which I am tempted to wear at times to this day, and I am grateful for many other things she did, as well. When I was able to get out a bit, after being home from rehab, she would encourage me to put on makeup, take me to the movies, take me to lunch and bring me ridiculously expensive jeans with which to flaunt my anorexic figure. You have to love a friend who's a fashionista -- even when you can barely take a shower -- forget about wearing makeup.

Glenn was there for me in a different way, and the truth is, if I had to put my money on who will be there, regardless of my circumstances, it would be Glenn -- ditzy, quirky, irresponsible Glenn. All I wanted during my illness and recovery was to feel something close to normal, again, but normal seemed an eternity away. Glenn helped me to focus on the things about which normal people obsess. She'd point out that my toes needed to be done, or that I was going to have to do something about the one hair that grows on my chin. You cannot imagine the frustration of not being able to address those seemingly inconsequential things on your own. Surely, every woman has at least one hair that grows somewhere you can't stand. If it hasn't happened to you, yet -- just wait. That friend, who will pluck it for you without asking, is a keeper. I have given strict orders to my closest friends and sisters-in-law to take notice and pluck that damn hair, should this ever happen, again.

My brothers were all so great. They were very patient and tried hard to help me while I was lying in the hospital room, as well as when I was lying in a bed in the middle of one of their living rooms. When someone lets you do that, you know where you stand, or more accurately, lie.

Tim Jr. was the closest of my siblings to me, and with him being 18 months younger, I had always been his protector. How the tables were turned when I got sick! He'd bring me peace of mind by cleaning my feeding tubes, wiping nastiness from my nose and monitoring my meds, an overwhelming task for my parents; and he'd read Oprah magazines to me to bring some peace to my soul. He would bring someone in to do my nails, something for which I was very thankful, as my mother wanted to do them for me and, God love her, I would rather not end up with them colored cotton candy pink or blood red.

Aunt Courtney would come and give me foot rubs; Roberta, and her husband, Jack, did the same. There were just so many wonderful people around me, like Jeanne and her husband Hal.

Jeanne, a strikingly beautiful, older woman, had entered my office, and my life, one day in November 2003, two and a half years before the divorce and my illness. I was in Concord Center, when I had run in to grab some paperwork, my three children in tow. She told me she had been given my name by the mother of a former intern of mine, who suggested I might need some help with shopping and gift-wrapping during the holidays. Boy, did I ever!

I asked her if she could return the next day, as I had my three cherubs with me. She agreed and, when we met, it was as if I had known her for decades. Not only did she help me that year with my holiday shopping, but she also suggested some decorating ideas for my office that I simply didn't have time to get around to doing. From that moment, she was a key player and force to be reckoned with, when Matthew and I did an extensive renovation on our house -- sadly, just prior to our separation.

I spent two days each week with Jeanne, receiving an education in classic design, while accompanying her on house tours, museum tours and to nearly every retail store on the eastern seaboard -- all to assist me in honing my own design sense and creating a beautiful environment for myself and my family. She gave me an education and friendship that I will forever cherish. When I met her, it was love at first sight. She has been an asset and inspiration to me from Day 1.

J.C., who had been more of an acquaintance, was right there when I needed someone to pick me up from that ill-advised trip to Atlantic City, prior to my near-demise. Right there, she remained. I had given her a fairly good head start in her real estate career by listing my house with her, but the friendship she extended went beyond obligation or gratitude. To me, that house was unsettled; I had sensed this from the beginning. No amount of renovations could fix it. At the very least, everyone who has moved in there, including me, has gone to extreme measures to change it -- through renovation, repair or expansion -- and it's ended up looking like a monstrosity. That house really is a metaphor for everything that went wrong in my marriage. Nevertheless, it brought me J.C.

Sometimes, the very best expression of friendship comes from someone you don't know. I have experienced this personally in my life on at least three separate occasions -- and all three of those occasions involved the gift of life. When that happens, you can't go through life without believing that we are all -- in some way, shape or form -- connected. The kindness of strangers should never be underrated or taken for granted. For example, although my daughters' birth parents are complete strangers, they gave me something no one else could, and I will be forever grateful for the beautiful gifts of Catherine and Savanah.

The precious gift of my own life, I owe to Eleana -- my organ donor -- and her family; people I did not know gave me the gift of friendship that I treasure most. One of them I will never know in body, but I am forever connected with her. My fate in life is a direct result of hers, and the strength and generosity of her family.

One of the things I wished for most was to be able to thank my donor's family for their immeasurable, life-altering gift. I wasn't sure if the laws allowed for that or if my wanting to say "thank you" would just cause them more pain. If I came out of this whole experience learning one thing (though believe me, I've learned many), it is that organ donation is a selfless act by the individual, who makes that decision, and a tremendous gift by the family, who ensures that the decision is carried out.

Giving is not easy and, truthfully, being on the receiving end of the gift of life isn't easy, either. I was completely overwhelmed by the things that had happened to me and the blessings I had received --

along with the guilt, sadness and heartbreak that intertwined with my gratitude and joy.

In the months and years that followed, I did develop a relationship with Eleana's family, through letters and email. In December 2011, the meeting I dreamed of came true and I met my donor family, face-to-face.

I took my son, Nathan, with me, and off we went to, finally, see my organ donor's family. Nathan and I were having some challenges getting along, and I thought it would be good to have some mother and son time. My only regret is that I did not bring my two girls to experience this once in a lifetime connection with total strangers, whose daughter's liver now resides in my body.

We flew from Boston, through North Carolina, to Tennessee, where I rented a car and drove 80+ miles to the Appalachian Mountains. I was planning on meeting Eleana's mother, step-father and her two young children. On our way, we stopped at Wal-Mart to get gifts for Eleana's two children and made our way to our hotel.

Eleana passed away after a car accident on May 21, 2005, just one day prior to my liver transplant, leaving behind an 18-month baby girl, Iliana, and a three year old son, Jackson. She was 21 years old.

As we got closer to our meeting time with them, my anxiety level increased dramatically. We were to meet at a local high school, where the Tennessee Organ Bank would be attending, along with community members and extended family and friends. What could I possibly say to this family for their daughter, sister, mother's gift of life -- to me -- a total stranger? How could I express my deep gratitude and appreciation for this amazing gift Eleana had given me?

I hoped the words would come to me. However, as I stood outside the high school, I felt nauseous. I was overwhelmed with the significance of meeting Eleana's still grieving family. Thankfully, a representative from the Tennessee Organ Bank met me in the parking lot and reassured me that, yes, it would be emotional, but Eleana's family was looking forward to meeting me, and they were inside waiting.

Nathan had great words of advice and said, *"Mom, just be yourself and everything will be OK."* We walked through the doors and I was immediately met and embraced by Melody, Eleana's mother. I felt an overwhelming back and forth of unspoken love between us. How can anything good come from something so horrific -- a child's premature death? Organ donation might be the only positive that can come from such a tragedy, and everyone in her family and at the event, conveyed that feeling.

Nathan met Eleana's two young children, who were absolutely adorable and so accepting of me. Her oldest, Eleana's son Jackson, had memories of his mom and it was obvious he wasn't quite sure of how much her life had impacted mine. Iliana seemed to only recognize the photographs of the beautiful young woman who was her mother.

There are no words big enough to thank someone for the gift of life, and I probably said that several times during our meeting. Melody had put together a slide show of Eleana's short life that was heart-wrenching. Eleana's stepfather, Fred, shared what he remembered of Eleana growing up, along with the trials and tribulations of her teenage years. Eleana's two small children listened, and Jackson cried through much of the slide show, and while hearing his grandpa tell stories of his beloved mother.

I got up to speak about my gratitude toward Eleana and her family, for offering me the most precious gift one could ask for -- an organ that was vital for my survival. There was a brief reception afterwards. I met Eleana's friends, who were still grieving tremendously, and some of their children, as well. Eleana's sister and her children were there, along with her extended family, in addition to community members -- including another liver transplant recipient.

Life is interesting when you can feel the amazing connection between total strangers -- who, through their life decisions, have enhanced yours -- unbeknownst to them. I feel this connection with my adopted daughters' biological parents, as well.

Nathan and I said our goodbyes that evening, and were physically and emotionally drained when we returned to our hotel. We had a quick dinner, and got some sleep, before making the journey back home.

Meeting Eleana's family has been such a cherished gift. We talk frequently, and I hope to have her children come visit for a couple of weeks this summer. Honestly, I feel an obligation to do more with my life, now that I've been given a second chance, by someone I didn't ever have the pleasure of meeting.

Life is so odd sometimes. Today, I feel differently toward just about everything. *Things* don't matter. I realize how little I need to survive. I'm content with very little, and what I hold as meaningful, I have in abundance -- my family, my health, my friends, and my appreciation of life.

I have something most people don't ever get during their lifetime -- I got to see just how much I mean to some of the people in my life. It is truly a gift to know, while you are still around to know it, who loves you unconditionally.

You have heard the expression, "With friends like these, who needs enemies?" I no longer have friends like those.

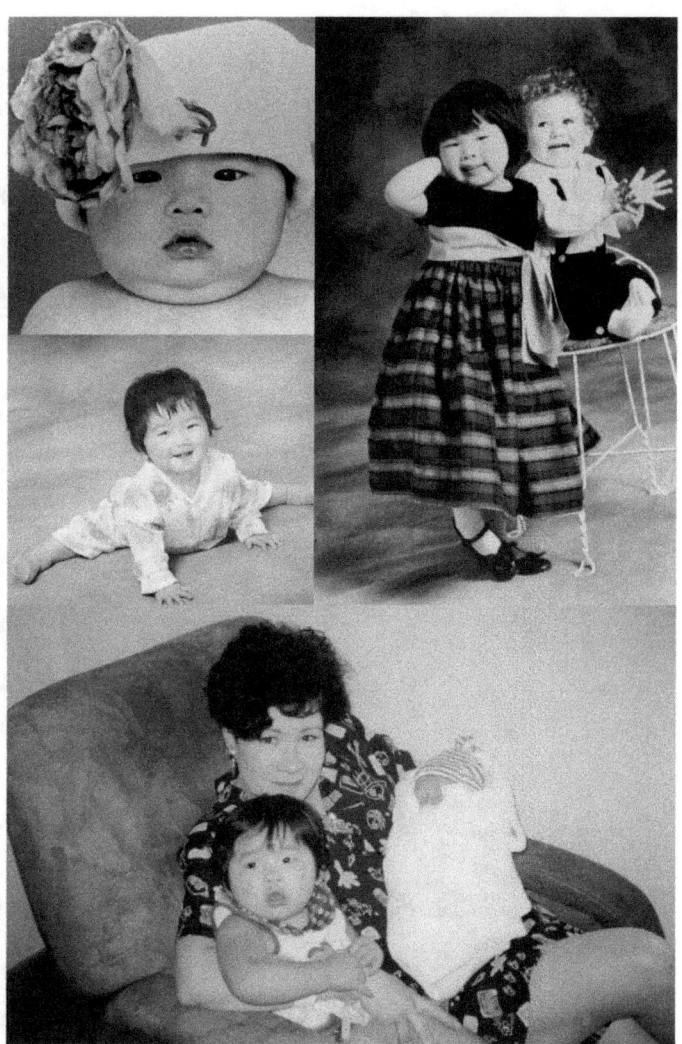

Clockwise, from top left: *Catherine (6 months) in 1996; Catherine (3) with Nathan (17 months) in 1998; Nancy with Catherine (2) and newborn Nathan in 1997; Savanah (10 months) in 2000.*

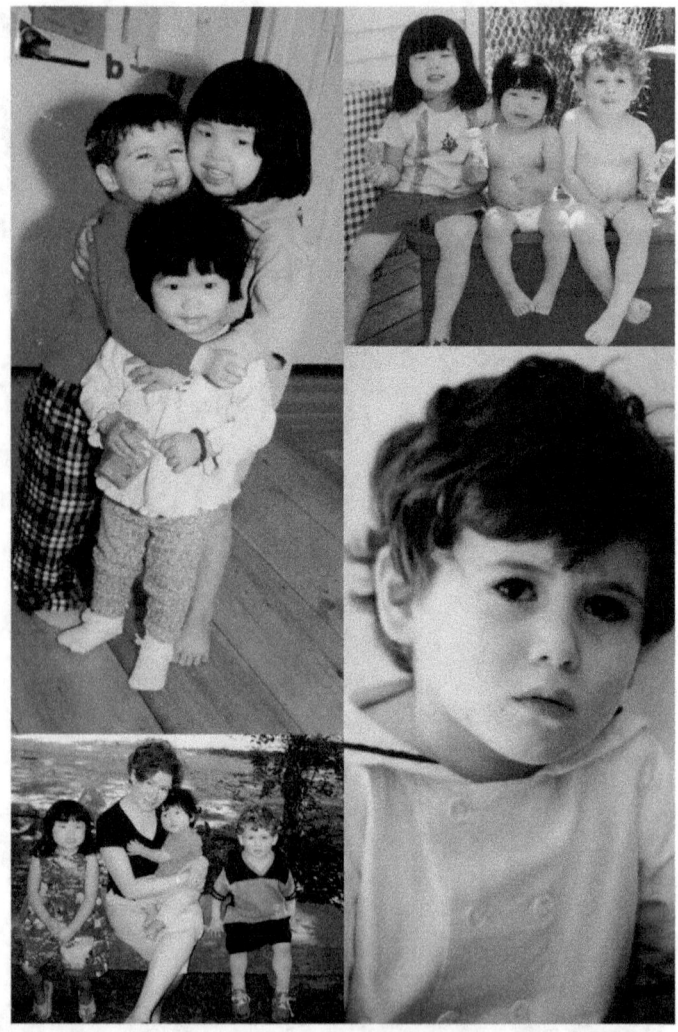

Clockwise, from top left: Catherine (5), Nathan (3) and Savanah (20 months) in 2001; Catherine (6), Savanah (2) and Nathan (4) in 2001; Nathan (5) in 2003; and Nancy with the children in 2001.

Top: At Beth Israel Medical Centre in 2005; ***Bottom:*** 2008

Clockwise, from top: *Fred and Melody, donor's parents; donor's daughter, Iliana; Nancy with Melody; Nathan (L) with Jackson, donor's son. All photos: 2011.*

Top: *Nancy at the Rose Bowl parade, 2012;* ***Bottom:*** *Nancy, reinvented, in 2010.*

CHAPTER 6

HOMEWARD BOUND

So, maybe, my parents had been right, after all, in making me take that shopping trip to Rindge. In a way, it was just what I needed, though not in the way they'd thought, I'm sure.

The outing had inspired me. It led me to reflect on the life I had left behind -- or rather, the life that I'd lost. I decided that I wanted it back. I missed my kids so much; I missed having my own home and being in charge of my own life. I missed my friends! Oh, how I longed for my friends, and for girl time that I really believed would take my mind off my troubles for a while. I was about to embark on a new life, one I could live as a single woman, starting over and gaining strength, slowly but surely. Of course, my mother was less than thrilled when I told her about my decision to find my own place. How else could she have felt, given my condition? In truth, she was probably right. However, even though my recovery was slow, I needed the encouragement of believing that I was ready to live alone.

I was only growing more and more disheartened and depressed at my parents' house -- and not just because of all the stuffed peppers. I felt so bad about relying on my mom and dad for absolutely everything, and I desperately wanted to be near my kids. I missed my life in Concord, and I missed Catherine, Nathan and Savanah more than I had ever imagined possible.

So, with all of my emotional baggage -- and medical paraphernalia -- in tow, I convinced my mother and my realtor, J.C., to help me look for an apartment. What an experience! My poor mother was, naturally, expressing many protective concerns and gave J.C. her list of conditions I needed.

"Nancy can't be on the second floor; she can't climb stairs."

"We need to find a ranch house, so she'll be all on one level."

"She has to have an attached garage, so she doesn't have to walk from the street."

Wow, attached garage. I figured I'd feel fortunate if I remembered how to drive by the time I was physically able to even try. At this stage, I couldn't even get my ass in and out of a car without the help of a hydraulic lift, or some brave soul who was willing to literally push me out of the vehicle. No kidding.

Oh, yeah, about the driving thing -- in addition to all of my other ailments, I was also suffering severe bone and joint pain, caused by a reaction to two medications that were not agreeing with one another. There was no way I would be able to drive until that condition was corrected and I couldn't figure out how I'd live on my own without driving. Moreover, it was no fun having to acknowledge that my mother was right. Yet, another mental setback, but I persevered.

In weighing all of my options and everything that had already happened, I decided that I was not going to add to my pain by continuing to be kept apart from my kids. The divorce proceedings were hell; obviously, so was my physical nightmare. Getting well was a long, hard road, and my babies were the beacon at the end of it. I was going to get back to them, whatever it took.

When we finally found an apartment that met my mother's requirements, I had plenty of help getting settled. My parents and brothers, and some friends from Concord -- so many people were terrific about helping me get moved.

I was moving from four different locations. At that point, I had possessions in my marital home; my office was being stored in my dad's friend's warehouse, along with the contents of my previous short-lived apartment rental; the things at my parents' home; and the hospital paraphernalia I was transporting back and forth. I needed a moving company -- and, fortunately, I had a great one in Glenn's friend Martin, and his family.

Everyone hates moving; it is just no fun. Even if you are going to your dream home, moving still sucks. The packing, the planning, and all the preparation is overwhelming. The only fun part is the pizza and beer, afterward. Although I wasn't doing any of the heavy lifting, even pointing to where I wanted the furniture to go was an enormous effort that wore me out. Besides that, my new liver was not ready for beer, and I couldn't get the pizza through my feeding tube.

However, I have to admit that once I was in and everyone had gone home, I had real mixed feelings about the whole endeavor. I sat on the sofa, looked around the apartment, and thought, *"Nancy, what the hell have you done?"*

I was utterly exhausted, barely able to get myself into bed that night. Once I lay down, my mind was filled with worry. Had I made a mistake? If I had, would I be able to admit it? I had bucked my mother's objections and my own trepidation. So many people had taken the time to help me get here. Now what?

Well, the next day I decided *now what*. Now, I would make it work -- plain and simple. Since my primary reason for moving had been to be nearer to my children, they received my total focus.

I didn't have to cook for myself, so that was energy I could conserve for another task. I could watch all the mindless television I wanted, without some well-meaning doctor idiotically forcing me to watch doom-and-gloom news stories. No feeling guilty about the Lifetime Movie Network! Since I couldn't drive, I didn't have to run any errands or drive carpool for the kids.

Life Lesson #31:
Stop concentrating on what you cannot do and find something, anything, for which to be thankful.

In all honesty, though, the driving thing was really a pain in the ass. It meant that I had to be really organized, so I did not burden anyone else with having to run extra errands for me. In spite of my dad's love of aimless driving, having him run all over Concord on my behalf was not what I wanted. It was enough that my parents came from Barre every week to take me to my scheduled medical appointments; I did not feel good about them having to do much more than that.

One week, though, they arrived to find me sick with exhaustion. I felt nauseous and utterly wiped out. Their parental radar kicked in and, realizing that I was overwhelmed with keeping up even my modest little apartment, they stayed later to do laundry, straighten up, and buy groceries. I was too tired to argue; in truth, I was very glad they did.

Organizing, ordering and picking up my medicines were daunting tasks, let alone separating them into their respective time blocks and boxes, to be sure I took the right ones at the right times. It was disconcerting at first, but I soon fell into a regular pattern of building this activity into my life -- as it remains to this day.

And so it went. I continued working toward recovery, and at last, I could be with my kids. Matthew and I agreed on a schedule that let me see them every day after school; they stayed with me on weekends. In the afternoons, Nana Roberta was also present. I was so grateful that she was able to be there to help me -- as much as I wanted to be with the kids, I was terrified of being too weak to handle the visits. Roberta was my backup, if I needed it; kindly staying in the background when she saw that I was doing okay. Her comforting presence also helped the kids to feel more at ease with my condition.

Some days, the kids came to my apartment; other days, I went to Matthew's house. I would help them with their homework and we would have dinner together. Then, I would head home before their father arrived. The visits were exhausting, yet, they were the high point of every single day. The kids were great; they understood how tired I was and were okay with me, occasionally, going to bed before they did.

The only sad -- and, therefore, negative -- part of the visits was that they did not include Savanah. After having seen me in the hospital, my poor baby remained traumatized by my condition and all the trappings that came along with it. Of course, I understood, but I was heartbroken. I hated that my child was afraid of me, and I hated that I could not hold her and make her fear go away. After all the nightmares I'd made better over the years, it was horrible to realize that this time, I was the monster. Who could blame her? I was not the mother she remembered, and I was scary and foreign to her.

However, I could not let my sadness over Savanah color the time I spent with Catherine and Nathan. I never said a word to them about how terrible I felt; I would have done anything to avoid making Savanah feel guilty, on top of being afraid. No, I made the choice to have fun with my two kids and to make the most of each of our visits.

We did have a good time together. After having spent so long apart from them, it was such a joy just to be in their presence. Without having to think about work -- or anything else at all, really -- I had so much more patience and genuinely appreciated Catherine and Nathan. That is something that doesn't always happen when you're juggling kids, a marriage, a home and a job.

We cooked together and, although it was fun, it often wound up being more work than help for me. Nevertheless, that was fine. It was the time together, the sharing a simple task, that mattered. We went for walks -- short, slow walks -- but the combination of fresh air and their laughter did wonders for my recovery. Catherine even made friends with a girl who lived with her mother in the apartment above mine. I began to realize that we had created a nice, easy life, free of the craziness of over-scheduling and wanting too much.

Life Lesson #32:

Remember these simple times, and resist the temptation to dive right back into being too busy. Instead, appreciate making pasta with your kids.

However, there is always another side to the story, isn't there? It usually is not pretty. The other side of my story was fighting Matthew to regain custody of the children. Although the end goal was, certainly, worth it -- having my three kids living with me, again -- the custody suit took every ounce of strength that I didn't give directly to the children.

Initially, the entire custody situation baffled me. It made perfect sense for the kids to have stayed with Matthew while I was in the hospital and during my recovery, but why did he pursue gaining custody when I was better? After all, he had not wanted custody when we had separated. It took some time, but I finally figured it out. Being a full-time father turned out to be much easier than he initially thought.

When I got sick, Matthew was involved with Kim, who was a licensed day-care provider. Their relationship was still fairly new, and I assume that she would have done anything to please him. He also had Nana Roberta, who would have done anything for our kids. Therefore, in essence, he had a tremendous support system, and it was no wonder he thought he could pull it off alone.

Indeed, this same man had told me, as I was scrambling to care for three toddlers, that he would probably be a better father when the kids were older. I suppose, in a sense, he was true to his word. Go figure.

What really killed me, though, was that he continued the custody fight, after it was clear that I'd eventually get well and be able to take care of the kids, again. I couldn't believe that he was so mean and hurtful. I had a full dose of anger and rage going, and decided I had better use it to keep myself energized for the fight.

I felt torn, during this time, uncertain of so many things. Of course, I wanted my children back -- nothing would change that. At the same time, I still felt physically weak and had doubts about my ability to fully care for them. I was putting on a brave face and acting as if I was completely confident, when I was not anywhere close. I couldn't help feeling that, if Matthew had been at all reasonable and kind-hearted, he'd simply have told me to take the time that I needed to heal and then we'd go back to our original parenting schedule.

During our divorce proceedings, the fighting, anger, and sadness had consumed me. Nevertheless, I had been somewhat healthy then. Now, I was going through it all over, again, with a mere fraction of the physical strength I'd had the first time around. However, I was hell-bent on keeping my children from knowing what was going on between their father and me. Divorce makes kids feel guilty enough. No way was I was going to let them know we were now fighting over them.

I put on my happy-mommy face and made the most of every single visit. Really, Nathan and Catherine were terrific. I guess they had missed me a lot, too, and were happy to be slowly getting their mother back. They both wanted to help me. They really pitched in -- even when I did not want them to help quite so much.

At one point, I had to wear Dynasplint braces, futuristic-looking contraptions intended to straighten out my arms. After being in a coma, the body has a natural tendency to return to a fetal position. Who knew? My physical therapist did a lot of work on straightening my arms, but wanted me to sleep in the braces to keep my arms from curling inward, again.

Lucky me, I had little Nurse Catherine to help. She was determined and strong but, unfortunately, not all that gentle. She was trying to be such a big help, but I would see stars as she worked those braces onto my arms. Maybe, unintentionally, she was a little more like Nurse Ratched, from the novel *One Flew Over the Cuckoo's Nest*, without the sadistic streak. It was all I could do not to scream sometimes, but I wouldn't have hurt her feelings for anything. For the record, my arms still aren't really straight today – although, Catherine did her best to make them otherwise.

As I began to feel stronger and started cooking more, Catherine also became my food critic. One of her favorite dishes was pasta with mozzarella, fresh basil and tomato, fortunately, something that was incredibly easy to make. Even the kids' involvement in preparation didn't slow me down too much. They liked feeling that they were helping me, so I was thrilled to find something we could all prepare together.

I experimented with other recipes; one of the best was beef with mushroom soy sauce, which got a rave review from Catherine. *"Mom, this is so good! You should open a restaurant and just serve this."* If only life were that simple, my child.

Somehow, we made it through those first months in my new place, through the custody war and all it entailed. Wait a minute. Not "somehow." I know exactly how. We made it through by sheer force of will and intense mother-love. We made it because we had to, because not making it was never on the table.

Finally, after 18 months of my battle with illness, losing custody of my babies and a pending divorce, I was granted primary custody of my children. Yes, I was still recovering and still weak, but hearing the judge's decision gave me more strength than I would have thought possible, at the time. The icing on the cake of having regained custody, was that my little family would now be complete -- Savanah came home. The greatest joy of my life -- aside from the simple fact that I'm still living it -- has been the reunion with all of my children.

I thought the pure joy would kill me. Okay, I was still nervous, but Nathan, Catherine and I had done pretty well together, so, I felt confident that things would be good now with the addition of Savanah.

My focus next shifted to Savanah's needs. As happy as I was that she was coming home, I was truly afraid of scaring her, and knew that I had to make a couple of decisions to protect my baby girl. First, the damn feeding tube had to go. I mean, really, what child wants to look at their mother with a tube hanging out of her nose? I am still amazed that it didn't freak out Catherine and Nathan, too.

My doctor was none too pleased, when I told him that I wanted the tube removed from my nose and surgically replaced into my stomach. He strongly advised against it, warning me that it could lead to infections or other complications. However, I was getting my way, even if I had to rip the disgusting thing out myself. The doctor, reluctantly, agreed to the procedure.

Next up was my lovely shaved head. I had the wig that Susan had bought for me, but didn't wear it all the time, since I didn't really see much of anyone. Savanah actually made me wear it to sleep. She just could not bear to see my bald head, and worried about what would happen if she came into my room during the night and saw me, sans hair. She would come in and straighten out the wig -- while I slept. I know she was scared, but honestly, how adorable is that?

Even though Nathan, my sweet and naive little guy, wasn't afraid of my appearance, he still had his opinions. Once, when he walked in on me naked -- trust me, quite by accident -- he said, *"No offense, Mom, but I liked your old body better than your new body."* No worries, son, so did I.

Overall, the kids and I were making a go of it, and Matthew and I worked out our visitation arrangement. The summer after the kids came home, I rented a house for us in Sacket's Harbor, in upstate New York, where we stayed for three weeks, relaxing on the porch that overlooked Lake Ontario. What a perfect little vacation -- except for one day in particular, when Matthew called. After talking with Catherine, Matthew asked to speak with me; he told me that he was putting money in my checking account so I could buy the kids the things they needed for going back to school.

"Great. Thanks. *I appreciate it, and know they do, too,*" I replied, trying hard to keep the snarky tone out of my voice. I figured he expected an overabundance of gratitude for helping me to clothe our children for school.

He responded, "Yeah, well, tomorrow I have to go for a colonoscopy." A colonoscopy is a medical test in which the doctor views the inner lining of the rectum and colon by inserting a long, tubular instrument with a camera attached. The patient usually receives an anesthesia of some sort in order to "sleep" through it and have no memory of the procedure.

Now, this caused a little internal conflict for me, a kind of angel-on-one-shoulder-devil-on-the-other situation. The old me (that would be the devil), could not help but feel that, after a liver transplant and brain surgery, a colonoscopy was like a freaking paper cut. So, the father of my children -- the man who never visited me after my surgery, and who fought me for custody of my children -- had to have a hose shoved up his ass the next day. Hmmm, I could really have had fun with this. I will admit that for a tiny second (or two), my mind did go there.

Bless that angel on one of my shoulders. She just would not let me stay in that frame of mind long. No, that darned angel kept interrupting the list I was mentally compiling of nasty things I could say about Matthew's medical procedure. Instead, after a reflective afternoon on the porch, I came to some interesting conclusions.

After everything I had been through with Matthew, I should not have been surprised by, what I saw as, his lack of compassion. Throughout the custody suit, he repeatedly made things more difficult for me than they had to be. We saw a mediator to work out a detailed parenting agreement, and even with that, he pushed the limits. He would sign the kids up for activities without letting me know, or change the plans for visitation, after we had agreed upon the arrangements. His excuse was that he had left me a message, when in reality he'd call our au pair to tell *her* about the change, not *me*. In retrospect, I guess that is all part of his controlling nature.

However, I must be honest and acknowledge that there is another part to his nature, as well. After all, I did love Matthew once and married him, with every anticipation of spending our lives together. Surely, I thought he had good qualities then, and I am happy to say now, that I was right.

In an earlier chapter, I said that I am grateful to Matthew for our children, and that is true beyond measure. He has other qualities I'm thankful for, as well, though many are connected to the children. As I see it, when you commit to someone for life, you hopefully base that commitment on physical or emotional attraction, and look for signs that your partner will exhibit certain qualities.

When Matthew and I married, I looked to him to be a good partner, parent, provider and protector. Although our partnership ultimately failed, for some time, he had all of those positive attributes. I expected him to be supportive in all the ways that mattered to me -- emotionally, professionally and personally -- and to respect and nurture my wants and needs. For the most part, he did. I even wonder, if by not telling me his wish that he wanted me to be a stay-at-home mom, was just really his way of supporting my career at the time.

Of course, I wanted and expected comfort "in good times and in bad." While our marriage was good and healthy, we shared that comfort. It cannot be expected to continue, once things go irreversibly wrong, but yeah, we had it once upon a time.

Another thing Matthew and I had, was fun. We shared many interests, things like love of art, films, travel and adventure. We enjoyed trying new restaurants and visiting new places. When I made my bucket list, I realized how strange it was that Matthew and I had never taken the Sundance trip together, given our mutual love of films. In retrospect, I think we would have had a great time.

Looking back, I can honestly say that Matthew and I shared many wonderful things. Our marriage was good for most of its 16 years, which is more than many divorced couples can say. Yes, things got ugly for a while, but overall I think we came out on the right side of things. Matthew is a terrific father, who supports our kids in every way in which they need him. Yes, sometimes I do get the occasional urge to criticize, but hey, I am human. It is those moments, when I most want to take a jab at his expense, that make me take a step back, instead, and consider the things I do appreciate about him.

So, sitting on my porch, looking out at Lake Ontario, I realized that not only had I chosen Matthew because of the good qualities he possessed, but that those same qualities were still what mattered to me. I also realized that I had my children now, again, and was well on my way to better health. I had a home. I had a job that I loved. I began to think that; maybe, it was time to add a personal life to that list. Perhaps, I was ready to put my list of good qualities to work, again, and try to restart my life.

CHAPTER 7

WHERE THE BOYS ARE

What could be worse than getting divorced, almost dying, and losing everything I had fought my whole life to build? That would be, accepting the fact that I was single.

What a wake-up call that was. Once I was back on my feet, literally, and in my own home with my kids, it hit me -- hard -- that I was alone, without a partner. Of course, I was elated to have my kids, and there would never be a choice between them and any man in my life. But, why should I have to choose? Why couldn't I have both my children and the company of a man?

I didn't necessarily want a man to become part of my children's lives so soon, after we were, finally, a family living under the same roof, again. Nevertheless, there was no reason that I could not have a life of my own, when the kids were with their father. I liked the idea. The only problem with meeting this goal was the need to actually get out there and meet someone.

It had been a long time, since I had tried to meet men. I thought about asking my friends if they knew anyone, but figured that, since most of them were married or seriously involved, the guys they knew were likely to be married, too. I was not interested in playing that game.

Another problematic side existed, about asking married friends for dating recommendations. Let's face it; married couples are not usually all that thrilled about having a single, available woman over for a fun-filled, kid-free evening. I do not care how close you are, it can be a threat. Girl friends' husbands want to stay as far away as possible from the conversation of dating, lest they appear too interested in my social life. Unless someone volunteers to introduce me to that great guy, with whom their husband works, I'd rather not get involved.

Why not go to a bar or a club, you ask? Ugh, that was the worst. Are there any clubs that play music for 40-somethings? Where was the nice jazz club that I thought would attract like-minded men? All I could find were dance clubs, and this 40-something was not happy about shaking it with a bunch of 20-year-olds. However, I did give it the old college try, and even dated a cute younger man, for a short time. The best thing that came of that was realizing that I'm not interested so much in the May-December romance; at least not when I'm the December. Texting 17 times between 12:54 a.m. and 5:13 a.m. made me come to my senses and realize I had three children, and didn't need a fourth. Actor Ashton Kutcher, you are hot, but I am suddenly a skeptic.

Life Lesson #33:

Never date anyone under age 28. Thinking about being a cougar, and actually being one, are two different things. No good can come from a relationship with a 20-year spread between our ages -- my limit is 14!

I decided to try the bar where Glenn worked. Her place of employment is in a nice hotel, so I figured it was better than a nightclub, and might draw a more adult crowd. In addition, Glenn would be there. My friend Bethany came along for company, and we did attract quite a few men -- lots of conversation, lots of interest. However, you know what kind of men go to hotel bars? Married ones, traveling on business -- not for me.

I was back to Square One. I tried hard not to feel discouraged, but having nothing to do and being alone, weekend after weekend, gets old -- really fast.

Life Lesson #34:

Make plans before you feel lonely, but especially consider making plans on the weekends, when people are typically with the ones they love (or are loving the ones they're with). Too many weekends alone won't do a thing to improve your attitude.

After continued bitching and moaning among my friends, Glenn found what we thought just might be the answer. She saw an ad in the local paper, from a single guy who was looking for love. Funny, but I hadn't thought to try the personals; they just seemed so, well, impersonal. The ad said that a dating service would conduct interviews at a local hotel to find compatible women for their client.

Maybe it's my business training, but I actually thought that was a pretty good idea. Have someone else do the leg work and then the guy could decide from among the finalists. However, since I was on the other end, I was a bit uncertain. Wouldn't it be embarrassing to interview for a possible date with a total stranger? Just how desperate did that make me?

Oh, what the hell. After all the indignities I'd suffered in the hospital, I really had nothing left to lose. Therefore, I dressed to impress and headed to the Marriott Copley hotel in Boston. At least, they'd chosen a nice location, which I figured was a good sign.

Wrong again!

When I asked the front desk staff about the event, no one even knew it was happening in their hotel. I had expected to go to a conference room, but was, finally, directed to the bar area. Hmm, dating interviews in a hotel bar? I couldn't help but wonder if this guy was really married after all.

About 50 women had turned out for the interview, and we all stood around not knowing what to do, as the staff hastily shoved together a few tables. We sat down, waiting on our calls. The women involved with running the event were really nice -- to one another. The rest of us sat there watching them order drinks, without ever offering us anything. They barely acknowledged us, leaving us to sit there and wonder what was happening.

I was tempted to leave, but honestly, was too curious to see how this thing was going to unfold. While curiosity didn't quite kill the cat, it -- certainly -- didn't do a thing to uplift the self-worth or the spirits of anyone in that room. When the woman conducting the interviews, finally, began talking to us, her manner went beyond rude. She pointed to the attractive blonde next to me and said, *"If he's looking for (actress) Catherine Zeta-Jones, he's not going to call you."*

I couldn't have been more stunned -- until she next pointed to me and said, *"If he's looking for (another actress) Reese Witherspoon, he's not going to call you."* Was this woman serious? I felt as if she had slapped me. I was completely embarrassed to merely have attended this event, but way more so than I'd anticipated. I had expected some personal questions, asked in a private setting -- not a public humiliation. This witch actually asked one of the women if her boobs were real!

The entire event was a disorganized, poorly executed disaster. In addition to my personal disappointment, as a business executive, the dating service women appalled me by their lack of professionalism. Honestly, all they had to do was thank us for our time. From a professional perspective, it would have made sense to acknowledge each of us with a brief note, maybe mention that the dating service would keep us in their database. However, I never heard another word, after that night.

Aside from the human aspect, it is just good business sense to treat people well. After all, you never know where your next big client might come from. I was so upset by the whole experience that I wrote a letter to the woman who organized the event, voicing my disappointment. As tempting as it was to verbally slam her, I was very professional. I explained why I was displeased, and offered some helpful tips for a better way to run that type of event. I even included a copy of my latest book and offered to work with her, if she ever needed a business consultant.

So, the search continued. As often happens, love did strike from a much-unexpected corner. I had known Marcus for years, since the time I was still married to Matthew, and Marcus was still married to his former wife. We knew one another through business; Marcus is president of an association in which I'm active. We were both divorced when we ran into one another at an association event, and could not deny the mutual attraction.

Talk about a whirlwind romance. I was surprised by how hard I fell for him. Suddenly, this nice, good-looking guy became much, much more. It looked as though I really did want a relationship.

With him living in Minnesota, however, it was challenging, at best, for us to see one another on any regular basis. Nevertheless, while long-distance relationships can be trying, they can also be kind of hot. After all, the distance apart whipped up all this excitement and anticipation, whenever we planned a visit. The initial reunion, all the terrific sex to make up for our time apart, romantic dinners -- yeah, an upside to the situation, definitely, existed.

My first visit to Minneapolis was early in our relationship, before we'd yet slept together. Something told me that this time, we were on the same page about having a physical relationship, and I was really looking forward to some steamy romance.

A few days before the trip, I met with my support group for our regular Starbucks session. As I told them all about my plans, I began to realize how long it had been since I'd been in a relationship. Connie dropped some subtle hints about having my eyebrows waxed and getting my hair colored -- point well taken. Then the subject of birth control came up.

I have to admit that the thought never once crossed my mind. Was I ever out of the loop! I realized that my diaphragm probably wouldn't fit anymore because of the massive weight loss when I was sick, so I needed an alternative -- and quick.

Perusing the family-planning aisle at CVS pharmacy, I was pleased to find that the Today Sponge, which had once disappeared from stores, was again on the market. I decided that Marcus was definitely "sponge worthy," and bought a box. I was all set for my much-anticipated trip to the Twin Cities.

The first time with a new man should be memorable, something that you'll always look back on as very special. Well, my first time with Marcus was certainly memorable, but more as a comedy skit than a lovely romantic encounter.

The sponge seemed like such a handy little contraption. According to the instructions, inserting it was simple; just like inserting a diaphragm. It had a little string to tug, when it was time to remove it. What could be easier? Well, I'm, obviously, never one to do things the easy way. The damn thing got turned around and the string was no longer anywhere to be found. I decided to wait it out and figure a way to remove it later.

Then, I had a scary thought, while sitting there locked in the bathroom. What if I couldn't get it out at all and wound up with toxic shock syndrome? Next thought? Quite frankly, I've had more than my share of scary illnesses, thank you, and I didn't want to create another. In the meantime, Marcus was wondering what was wrong with me. I was clearly nervous and far from sexy. Embarrassed, I broke down and told him what was wrong.

After lying on his bed in a number of rather odd positions, I still couldn't remove the sponge. Now, I was really getting nervous, afraid that I was actually driving the sponge further inside my body, as I tried to remove it. In desperation, I got into Marcus's huge walk-in shower, where I behaved like a contortionist for a while, practically standing on my head. Still no luck.

At this point, I was seriously worried that I might be doing permanent damage to myself, so I bit the bullet and called the support number on the package. I tried everything they recommended and still could not get it out. Good Lord, just how far inside me could this thing have gone?

Think I'm embarrassed yet? Wait, it gets better. Without any options left, we headed to the local Emergency Room. Yup -- checked in and told total strangers that I couldn't remove my birth control device. To make matters worse, the attending physician was a man in his 30s. Of course he was. No such luck that I'd get a female doctor.

I was so mortified that I could not stop laughing. Seemed like a reasonable reaction to me. Not that I thought this was in any way funny. When my 30-something doctor heard why I was there, he said, *"Well, at least it's something that's supposed to be in there."*

That really put things in perspective. I could only imagine what manner of things this young man must see. Oddly enough, though, the paperwork they gave me when I left said, "removal of foreign vaginal object." I wonder what they write for women who lose their Ben Wa balls (a sex toy)...

So yes, the first time I slept with Marcus was quite memorable. Thank heaven for good old-fashioned condoms; at least we were able to salvage the rest of the trip, which was quite wonderful.

I don't think it matters how smart you are or how much you've gone through, when it comes to relationships and love, there's always a learning curve. Of course, I got caught up in the excitement of this new relationship and, once again, missed the signs of danger looming ahead. Some were subtle -- others, not so much.

One of the things I really appreciate is a man who is photo-ready when he leaves the house. Every girl is crazy about a sharp-dressed man, right? It became clear that Marcus's appearance was as important to him, as it was to me. Actually, more so. How many guys ask you which shoes match their new shirt? It is, maybe, not a major thing, but a sign, nonetheless.

Marcus's position, as president of the association -- of which we were both members -- caused some difficulties, too. I, initially, figured that being in the same field, we'd get bonus time together, when we'd both be attending the same events. Not so fast. Because of his high-profile position, Marcus felt it was inappropriate for us to share a room. The fact that he thought anyone cared just boggled my mind; in fact, I am pretty sure they assumed we were sharing a room, anyway, since we were clearly a couple. Hey Marcus, welcome to the 21st century.

I found it so odd. His family knew we were together and accepted me just fine. I could not understand why he was so skittish around our colleagues. He only seemed comfortable when we took a trip where we did not know anyone.

I tried to rationalize his behavior, and did a pretty decent job of it -- for a while. Then came the proverbial last straw. I was traveling to Minneapolis, where he lives, and he suggested that I get a hotel room. Excuse me, but your girlfriend is coming to town, and she can't stay at your home? That did it. Time for me to hit the road.

Now, we only see one another at speaking engagements, and it's usually awkward. Once I spent an entire trip listening to colleagues talk about the fabulous private parties they'd been invited to in Marcus's suite. Guess who didn't make the cut?

I don't need a brick wall to fall on me. Nope, just give me a few blatantly obvious signs indicating that things are not going to work out.

On my own, once again, I decided to try what I figured was the only option I had left -- the dreaded world of on-line dating. Let's be honest, I think all single women have, at least, thought about it at one time or another. In fact, I think on-line dating is becoming more of the norm for singles these days than unusual. Even before I was ready to take the plunge, it tempted me to just peek and see what -- or who -- is available on the Web. If you ever have insomnia -- and who among us single girls hasn't? -- you probably already know that lots of opportunities exist on-line to "connect" with a total stranger at 3 a.m.

So, once again, I said, 'what the hell' and flung myself into the electronic jungle. A jungle it is. Finding love in the 21st century is not easy. I really believe that women have a tougher time than men do, because, unfortunately, men in their 50s are looking for women in their 30s. So, where am I supposed to meet a guy -- in the geriatric ward?

I was kind of surprised by the fact that so many people seemed to want to be in really serious relationships -- does everyone in the world want permanence? I did meet some very nice men, who remain my friends today. But, I just wasn't interested in a total commitment.

As I see it, most single women in their 30s and 40s have the average 2.3 children in the picture. I'd figured that men, who were 10 to 20 years older, wouldn't be so interested in the total package of an instant family. Boy, was I wrong. I'd have two dates with a guy and he'd start talking about a long-term commitment.

One man I dated told me that, if we had sex, it meant we were in a big, committed relationship. What? I felt as if the tables had turned. It seemed so strange that the man was begging for a commitment, while all I was asking was to just date for a while, and enjoy the passionate expression of sex, without having to seal the deal. He was so relentless that I had to stop seeing him.

Where were all these commitment freaks when I was in my 20s and looking for the real thing? Back then, the guys in their 20s couldn't have cared less about commitment -- but they'd promise one, if it would get them laid. I guess, it's a classic case of things not aligning, at a time it works for you. I married the man who made that youthful commitment to me, and look where that ended -- with me trolling the Internet for a suitable stranger, who didn't want to tie me down.

Did I mention that it's a jungle out there? The on-line dating world is, absolutely, flooded with people, and it can be really hard to weed through the chaff.

Life Lesson #35:
Check out your on-line competition and act as a member of the opposite sex during the free trial. It's a good way to decide which sites offer the most options. Find out where you have less competition and join that site -- they'll be happy to see you.

So, I went on a few dates, having forgotten how exhausting it can be to make small talk with a virtual stranger over dinner. I met quite a range of men, I'll tell you. However, I was doing this on purpose, and with purpose, subscribing to a philosophy put forth by my friend, love mentor and dating expert, Dr. Diana Kirschner, in her *Dating Program of Three*. This is not the old school, go on three dates with a guy to determine if he's "the one" rule. Much more contemporary -- and more fun -- is Dr. Diana's approach, if you're lucky enough to find three men who you want to date and who want to date you, at the same time. The idea is to not have sex with any of them, but see all three sporadically over a period of time.

This way, you don't see any one of them too often, and if one isn't willing to hang around and go the distance, then he's just not that into you and not worth your single-focus, anyway. Dating three men at once also helps a woman to recognize and break those same destructive patterns that cause her to end up in nowhere relationships. In the long run, the juggling of men in the *Program of Three* helped me become more comfortable with dating in general, brought me self-esteem, fulfillment and more than a few funny stories to share with my support group -- and with you.

If any men should read this, I hope you'll take away this bit of advice, if nothing else. Do not talk about your ex beyond saying, "I'm divorced." Trust me, you don't make yourself look any better to your date by talking about what a bitch your ex-wife is. We get it. She's your ex; odds are that you don't think she hung the moon. Details about former marriages are on a strictly need-to-know basis, and no one needs to know -- certainly, not on the first date. If you're a widower, we're sorry for your loss, but if you can't get through an evening without extolling the virtues of the angelic late missis, you aren't ready for dating, yet.

In reality, we are all so busy, way too busy to tolerate someone else's drama. God knows, we have enough of our own -- with kids, families, jobs, homes, and bills. We already have deadlines to meet and demands to fulfill; we really don't need another person to take care of full time.

So, what's a woman to do? They -- whoever "they" are -- say that once you stop looking for it, love surprises you. However, can you really just stop looking?

Life Lesson #36:

While you're looking for love, take care of yourself. Schedule a massage and indulge in some intensive self-care. I know it may seem trite, but trust me --it isn't. When you haven't had any physical contact in a long time -- be willing to pay for it.

Personally, I think that love was either on vacation, or just really, really busy somewhere else, when I put my toe in the pond. However, I never stopped looking for it, because I knew it was out there, somewhere. One thing that I'd learned from my dating adventures, was to develop a better understanding of what I want, and for what I'm looking. I even have a slogan for it: "Live close; visit often!"

CHAPTER 8

LOVE HURTS

My return to the dating world made me realize something that I didn't really like to acknowledge -- I was tired. Gee, I wonder why?

That realization surfaced while Marcus and I were still together. All that traveling to maintain our long-distance relationship only added to my exhaustion. However, I jumped at Marcus's suggestion, when he said, *"Sweetness, I think you could use a massage."* Silly me thought this was his sensual invitation that meant, solely, to relax and seduce me. My reaction: *"Bring it on!"*

Once again, I misread the signs. Marcus had *not* been talking about hot oils and candles. Far from it.

He was talking about Rolfing, of which I had been blissfully unaware until he explained it to me. Really, that's just another way of saying I'd been ignorant and was about to get schooled.

"It's a new kind of massage therapy, Nance. I think you'd really benefit from it," he said. *"It's terrific. It will help with your posture -- straighten you out. You'll feel wonderful afterward."*

Rolfing is an aggressive form of massage. It's a somewhat unorthodox holistic system, in which a person's soft tissue is manipulated, to correct a neurological movement disorder. The disorder can be birth-related or caused by physical trauma, infection, poisoning or a reaction to pharmaceutical drugs.

During my illness and recovery, God knows I experienced my share of physical trauma and took a plethora of pharmaceutical drugs, not to mention my poor posture and a sedentary lifestyle, which could have created an unhealthy muscular condition in my body. Yes, my friends, the connective tissue in my body formed thick plates, called fasciae, which caused muscular imbalance, reinforcing bad posture and bad health. I hoped that Rolfing would remedy whatever caused my muscular condition and the resulting physical problems.

After Marcus addressed the finer points of Rolfing, I had to admit that it sounded tempting. You really want to believe that all those years of ignoring your mother's stern admonitions to "sit up straight" can be reversed, and that you will look and feel great -- and young -- again. So, what the hell, why not do it?

In truth, something about the idea of Rolfing did appeal to me. I knew, in addition, that recovering from the extent of physical trauma my body had endured was not a quick process. It was taking a long, long time -- much longer than I'd anticipated -- to really move beyond surgeries and recovery. Though, I will be forever grateful for the medical procedures and practitioners that kept me alive, and now kept my new liver functioning, I had a strong desire to do something to help myself.

Up to this point, I had no real input into anything that aided my recovery. I had to go to physical therapy; I will always have to take the meds. Not doing so would be idiotic -- if not suicidal. However, as Marcus explained Rolfing, I began to think outside the box. The more I listened, the more I realized Rolfing would give me action to take some control over my own recovery. I wouldn't have to rely solely on the tenets of western medicine, as much as I knew that they'd already helped me.

I saw that I had other options. Why not try a holistic approach to feeling my best? Why not expand my horizons and actively pursue a treatment that could benefit my body, mind and spirit?

What reason did I have not to take a chance on something new, that was going to help me feel great -- and in ten sessions, two weeks apart? This was, definitely, appealing to me. Since my surgery, it seemed to me that everything I'd been doing entailed my efforts to get back on track, back on top. Now, I was determined to go the final distance, to do whatever it would take to get my health back -- totally -- and to prove to myself that I could do it. I'd had two years of emotional and physical trauma, so I didn't think it could hurt to give Rolfing a try. Then again, I didn't think so many of the things I'd experienced over the past couple of years would ever have hurt me so much. You would think I'd have learned my lesson about what hurts. Wrong.

After listening to Marcus's wildly enthusiastic recommendation, I embarked on a little research, went on-line and found an adorable, 30-something Rolfing masseur. Enter the handsome Tad Roode.

You have no idea how ironic that name is -- but oh, you will. Irony and me are pretty good company. Nevertheless, back to Tad. I watched an informative video clip on his website, where he highlighted the benefits of Rolfing. He was engaging and compelling in his presentation that, as a business consultant, I naturally admired. Also, Tad was smokin' hot, which I also admired. His number flashed at the bottom of the screen. I mean, how often does a gal get a guy flashing his number for her to call him? The prospect of the arms, attached to that cute face, giving me a massage was too hard to resist. I contacted him, immediately.

It was perfectly harmless. What Marcus didn't know couldn't hurt him -- but it sure would end up hurting somebody. Wanna guess who? Me.

I got Tad's voicemail and left an embarrassingly enthusiastic message. He returned my call promptly, surely meaning he was just as excited to begin Rolfing me, as I was to have him do so. We scheduled our first session to begin in the summer. Marcus was happy that I had taken the initiative to book my first of 10 sessions. He assured me I would look and feel great, afterward.

Tad suggested that I wear a sports bra and underpants. No thong underpants? Leaving that thought behind, I arrived at Tad's condominium at 10 a.m. on the day of my first appointment.

"Hello, Nancy."

"*Holy crap,*" I did not say aloud, but that's what I exclaimed in my mind. He was even better looking than in his video clip.

I couldn't wait to get started. While Tad reviewed my body from nearly every angle, I struggled for pure thoughts. He was empathetic and encouraging, as we talked about my past physical and mental health trials and tribulations. So, he was good looking and a good listener to boot. It was Marcus's own fault if I ended up running off with this guy, as Tad began slowly and steadily pushing on my body. I was completely distracted by the way he looked in that ...OUCH!

"*Ummmm, Tad, is this supposed to feel this painful?*"

"*You're doing great, Nancy. This is good.*"

Okay, if he said so. I was on my way, and damn proud of myself for taking the first steps in helping my body heal from the trauma it had been through.

Session No. 1 -- Check.

Bring on Session 2.

Tad's dog greeted me when I arrived. He was adorable, just like his owner, and it was so cute how he slept on a pillow during sessions. I told Tad that seeing him with Boxer, his pet, almost made me want a dog of my own. Maybe I said that just to relate to him on a different level.

Life Lesson #37:

Remember, the things women do and think, when in lust, rarely reflect reality. Step back, take a breath, and listen to your head, before letting your heart get carried away.

I was flat on my back when Tad started working on my calves. I stifled screams, when he started to move around my soft tissue. Quivering in pain, my only relief came when I excused myself to relieve my bladder of the tea and water, which turned out to be not such a good idea, after all. I went to the bathroom five times.

But, once again, Tad was nothing but empathetic, despite the pain he had created. Such a great guy...

He mentioned that he'd seen the piece on television station FOX 25, about me and my illness, and told me he thought I was inspiring. That helped to inspire me to make it through the second session and all of that pain. I was sure Marcus had been right. Rolfing was going to help me, in more ways than one.

However, I was not recovering well from the pain, between sessions, and really was in physical agony. The way I saw it, one night after a session, I had two options -- I could either drive myself to the emergency room, or call an ambulance. It would be too embarrassing to answer all the nosy neighbors' questions if an ambulance pulled into my driveway. You'd think I'd have learned not to give a damn about what my neighbors saw by this point, but lessons that big take a long time to master.

The drive to the emergency room was ridiculous. I suffered excruciating pain every time I made a turn or came to a complete stop. It's a wonder I didn't kill myself on the way to the hospital. The emergency room nurse looked like she wanted to kill me, after hearing that my pain was the result of an elective massage session. She refused to do X-rays and sent me home. At least, the neighbors didn't know.

In another session, while Tad was honing his craft on my butt, he practically lifted me right off that table with his torture! I was groaning so loudly, the S.O.B. complained that his neighbors could hear me. *Did he really just say that?*

That was when I started plotting his demise. How could Marcus profess to love me and, at the same time, recommended such torture? I didn't know how much more I could take; my butt was on fire. I didn't think anything, except a laser torch, could make its way through the layers of my butt's fatty tissue, where my coveted fasciae laid waiting. But Tad, with his brutish fingers and arms, and ugly assed tattoo, was relentless. I sighed in relief when he left my butt behind and moved to my thigh. The sigh -- and the relief -- were short-lived.

OUCH!

Marcus must have a secret vendetta against me, I concluded. It was the only explanation, and in that moment, all my ravaged body wanted was to break up with him in the cruelest way possible.

"*You're doing fine. You will feel so much better after the 10 sessions.*" I heard Tad's voice; once sweet and buttery, now sounded like scratching nails on a chalkboard to me.

Yeah, I'll feel better when the 10 sessions are done – because I won't be your personal torture victim, any longer. Then, it occurred to me, I was actually paying this man to hurt me! Instead of having my body tortured on a dog-hair-ridden massage table, I should have been lying on a therapist's comfy couch, having my head examined!

Tad's dog met me at the door, on one particular day, with bared fangs and a mean spirit. He wasn't the only one. Tad had his own attitude. He was pissed because I had not called to tell him I'd be late.

I wasn't about to tell him that I couldn't call because I had to position my Blackberry under my tailbone, to alleviate the pressure on my butt, while I drove. My thong -- my personal rebellion against my tormentor -- held it in place.

I asked Tad if anyone ever referred another client to him. *"I sure won't,"* I said aloud, as he dug into me even harder.

Life Lesson #38:
When someone has the ability to cause you pain, it's best to keep the snide comments to yourself.

During the torture, Tad mentioned that he and his wife were about to leave for a two-week vacation in France. Bastard. He knew it would screw up the Thanksgiving deadline that I had set for finishing the sessions.

While he worked on my ribcage, where most of the scars from my transplant surgery are located, I writhed, until I could no longer tolerate the pain and had to take a break. I was beginning to wonder if, maybe, Tad was a serial killer, the type that likes to torture victims before putting them out of their misery.

Back on the rack, it was more of the same.

"Starting today, you should begin to feel better."

Liar. Sadistic freakin' liar.

I never felt better after seeing him -- only worse, much worse. Who was this guy kidding? Rolfing, at his hands, was like paying someone to beat you, until you felt unimaginable pain in areas that you never even knew existed.

Why hadn't I taken up something less painful, like ballroom dancing or yoga, or poking myself in the eye with a sharp stick? I had already experienced about as much torture as anyone should have to go through. The fact that I'd voluntarily signed up for this, was insane. Holistic my ass; "hellistic" was more like it.

Then, Tad left me a whiny, annoying voicemail, asking me why I had not scheduled my last two sessions. I didn't call back right away, because I only had the strength to lift the television remote to watch 11 straight hours of the HGTV channel. Nevertheless, I did schedule the last two sessions.

However, I decided to show Tad exactly what kind of pain he was putting me through. Okay, I was a little dramatic, but I had to get through to this guy, and he deserved the guilt!

I showed up at the next session in the wheelchair that I'd used after my surgery. Tad, the smug bastard, seemed to take it all in stride, which really pissed me off.

"*Don't tell me your other patients show up in wheelchairs, too?*"

"*Sometimes,*" he smiled.

I wanted to do physical damage to him, putting him in a wheelchair, right then and there!

Tad asked if he'd get to meet Marcus, and I told him, "*Absolutely. I'm booking Marcus a Rolfing session with you when he visits me in December, and I get to watch!*"

At one of the last sessions, I had taken an Ativan pill to relax me before I arrived, and was a little out of it. I told Tad I needed help to get to the bathroom and, on the way, managed to open the front door and let his stupid dog out.

Tad flew by me, yelling something about earplugs on the table. How thoughtful of him. There was construction in the neighborhood, and those would no doubt help me relax. I put them in and promptly fell asleep.

When I woke up 90 minutes later, Tad was nowhere to be found! Leaving the condominium, I found him and his dog asleep on the doorstep. I thought about kicking him awake, but figured his wife could have the pleasure, when she returned. That nap was, really, what I needed. For the first time, I left a session feeling great.

I realized the following Monday that, thank God, only two more sessions remained. I had pre-paid for them, which I guess was Tad's way of making sure I returned to his chamber of horrors, his dungeon of Rolfing.

It was during the time I was in Rolfing, that Marcus and I had begun arguing over the simplest things, which, I now know, was the beginning of the end. Good old 20/20 hindsight. That was when I was planning to visit, and he wanted me to book a hotel room, rather than stay with him.

What kind of man doesn't share his home with his girlfriend, the woman he says he loves, when she flies halfway across the country to see him? What kind of man does that?

I did not have time for that. Convinced that Marcus knew, down deep, that Rolfing was worse than the liver transplant and the recovery from it, I left him and never looked back.

By that point, I had also stopped driving myself to the Rolfing sessions, having full knowledge of the pain I'd be in, after Tad was done with me. To add insult to injury, my round-trip cab rides cost $197.

My debacle of vengeance hit its peak when I hired my 12-year-old daughter to make me a T-shirt, which read, *"I'd rather be Rolfing"* on the front and, *"I Stand Corrected"* on the back. As I arrived for my final session, I wore my T-shirt and thought Tad would just love the sarcastic humor in the simple, yet profound phrases. He never acknowledged my cleverness, which just further fueled my hatred of him. He never even noticed!

After the session ended, Tad said, *"Congratulations, Nancy. You've completed your goal!"*

Then, he asked me why it was so important to finish by Thanksgiving.

"Because now I can add never having to see you, again, to my list of things for which to be thankful."

Okay, I have something really funny to confess. For reasons I cannot at all explain, I -- somehow -- ended up loving the guy. I guess it's like that phenomenon known as the Stockholm syndrome, in which an abducted hostage develops a sense of loyalty to the kidnapper to survive, regardless of whatever abuse the hostage experiences.

Well, that's Tad and me. I can, actually, look back on the whole experience and appreciate what it did for me -- not to mention the laughter I experience about it, in hindsight. What kind of nut burger, however, puts up with this kind of torture, when in the middle of it, she can't possibly find any benefits of such an ordeal? Me! Did I mention that I don't like being a quitter? Like labor pains, I can forget and move beyond this one, stopping now and then to have some laughter, at my own expense.

Since the Rolfing, people do tell me my posture is better and that I've never looked better. I do feel healthier from it. In the end, I have to admit, that Rolfing did for me what I'd hoped it would.

Maybe, Tad isn't so bad after all.

CHAPTER 9

WHEN YOU WISH UPON A STAR

None of us, no matter how much we'd like to do it, can ever re-write history -- unless, of course, you're writing a work of historical fiction. While there have, definitely, been times when I've wished that the pain and agonies of my life were not real, I can honestly say that I would not go back and change a single thing. From Rolfing, to divorce, to even the transplant, every emotional blow, every physical ailment, every devastating detail of my life, has brought me to where I am today. Besides, I think I like it here.

Without being unable to conceive children, I would never know my cherished Catherine and Savanah. Without being able to conceive, I would never know the true miracle of Nathan. Without my divorce, I would never know what I really want in love and life. Without my illness, I would never know the real treasure of having one's health. Without my illness, I would never have realized how the limitless love of a parent doesn't end when their child is grown, and how true friends and family are the only things worth cherishing in life. Without my illness, I would never know -- down to my core -- how it is so much better to give than to receive, and how important it is to have an attitude of gratitude.

Without all I have experienced, I would never know that I am the luckiest person in the world.

I'm not saying that there haven't been times when I felt like "poor me" and asked, "Why me?" I've had my moments of self-pity and of feeling like a victim. I am so very human, as I think I've made fairly obvious in this book. Too obvious, perhaps! But, since I survived it -- divorce, coma, transplant, brain surgery -- I figured there must be reasons for it all. So, like any normal person who has been at death's door, but turned away for lack of a desire to walk through it, I decided to focus on re-entry into my life.

Lying in a hospital bed gives you a lot of time to think -- when you're not in pain, that is. I spent long stretches of time imagining the moment when I could make a plan that went beyond going an hour without throwing up. I spent long hours of rehab imagining the things that I wanted to do and the places I wanted to go, which helped to get me through many of those painful physical therapy sessions. I just kept envisioning the light at the end of the tunnel. Not *that* light. I wasn't going in that direction anymore, and I decided that since I hadn't kicked the bucket, there was only one sure thing I had to do. I made a bucket list.

My wish list was a compilation of all of the goals I wanted to achieve following my transplant. Honestly, I made it because I truly needed something to look forward to, and the inspiration to keep putting one foot in front of the other. A bucket list is a very personal thing, by the way. Some may shake their heads in wonder at the things another person yearns to do. I say, judge not.

With that caveat in mind, first up on my list was taking my kids to Disney World -- remember, judge not! How can you watch those commercials -- with the kids all giggling, unable to sleep because they're going to Disney the next day, and the camera cuts to the parents awake in their beds, giggling and excited too -- and not want to take your kids to the most magical place on earth? I mean, hey, it's the first thing all the Super Bowl's Most Valuable Players say they're going to do, after they've won the big game. It made perfect sense that it would be at the top of my to-do list, after I beat all the odds and won the biggest battle of my life.

So off we went, me, Savanah, Nathan and Catherine -- ages 7, 9 and 11, respectively, at the time -- and our new Mexican au pair (a nanny from a foreign country), Neena, who literally arrived just two days prior to our boarding the plane to Orlando. Good thing she came along with me. I swear that I must have been the only single parent to enter into the

Magical KingDumb (no, that's not a misprint, folks) that week.

I felt so out of place walking around that park and must admit that it was a bit of a bummer, at first. It seemed that everywhere I turned I bumped into couples --husbands and wives -- with their 2.3 children, most of them under the ages of my three cherubs. Why hadn't I brought my kids here sooner? How could I have deprived them of sharing the magic of Disney with both of their parents, for all these years?

But, as I began navigating my way through the park and the masses, it was easy to see that happily-ever-after was not the destiny of every couple in this, the happiest place on earth. You can learn a lot about relationships from standing in long zigzag lines and tuning into people's conversations. Even the body language at Disney struck me. For a place that is supposed to be where dreams really do come true, it looked to me like some of these people were living out a nightmare.

I remember one frustrated mom, suggesting that her hubby get in the line, where bags were being checked. Security, like everything at Disney, is abundant. As that husband joined the line, just ahead of me, his 2-year-old daughter ducked under the turnstile and bounced toward the entrance. As he made his way through, his wife pointed out that, *he was in charge of the toddler princess, who was now 50 feet ahead of them.* To which he exclaimed, *"You told me to go through the line where they check bags. I can't do two things at once!"*

Well, of course, he can't, I thought to myself. Even my 9-year-old son knows that. Nathan often remarks on a male's inability to perform more than one task at a time. We women, on the other hand, are naturals at multi-tasking. I think it's survival of the fittest. We recognize that men can't do two things at the same time; therefore, we become experts at it. We have no choice.

We did have our share of fun and magical moments at Disney, though. The kids really enjoyed themselves and even surprised me a bit. I hadn't expected, that at age 11, Catherine would thoroughly have a blast. She loved everything about the place and her excitement was infectious. Nathan, on the other hand, was a bit more reserved. He takes things very literally, and carefully read every warning sign he saw, which made him pass up several rides because of the potential hazards -- even though he was neither pregnant nor wearing a pace maker.

Know what part was magical for this Mommy? At Epcot and Universal, you can buy an adult beverage and carry it with you, while you walk around the grounds. Such a lovely way to soften the edges -- of what can be a harrowing experience.

I did get edgy at the sight of all those little girls in princess dresses, clawing their way to Cinderella's castle. It made me want to shake someone and ask, *"What message are we sending to our daughters (and sons, for that matter)?"* There is no Cinderella's castle, without a hell of a lot of great ideas, perseverance, smarts, opportunity and timing. Magic has nothing to do with it, though an inheritance might help. Listen, girls, you have a much better chance, of making that dream of living in a castle come true on your own, than you do waiting and hoping for your prince to come along. Wishing it, won't make it so.

It was all I could do, not to rip the dresses off those pre-school princesses, and tell them all to grow up and get over it. Why perpetuate the myth that "someday my prince will come?" He'll come, all right, but not in the way you'd like. Not on a white horse, in shining armor, with a castle and a promise to love, honor and cherish you. It just doesn't work that way -- trust me on this one. Of course, I didn't do or say any of that to all of those beautiful children with magic in their hearts and stars in their eyes. You'd have read about me a lot sooner, if I had!

Not to be forgotten is the lovely couple we met at the Pirate Dinner on our last night in Orlando. They were dressed as pirates and celebrating their 25th wedding anniversary. Apparently, this is an annual tradition for their every anniversary. The best part? They had no kids -- no need to, it seems to me. They're living out their own Disney childhood fantasies, as adults. To each his own.

As it turned out, the trip included yet another experience with someone, who seemed to have left the baby on the bus, as it were. We took a side trip to visit our au pair's aunt and uncle, who lived in Orlando. They were lovely people, who welcomed my kids and me into their home. We spent a pleasant afternoon in their company. It was nice to see Neena interact with her family; I was glad she was able to spend some time with them.

Her aunt gave us a tour of their house, and I commented on how lovely each room was, as we walked through the living room, dining room, kitchen, den, master bedroom...and nursery. Wait a minute. Neena had told me her aunt and uncle didn't have children. What she hadn't mentioned was that her aunt, apparently, didn't accept that fact. The nursery was a little girl's dream room, beautifully decorated, complete with the "child's" name stenciled on the wall.

I'll admit that my initial reaction was to think the woman was crazy, but -- ultimately -- I think it's sad. Here is a woman who clearly longs to be a mother, to the point that she keeps a room for the fantasy child. Out there in the world are so many real children who could benefit from her love and affection. I wanted, so badly, to talk to her about adoption, but I simply didn't know her well enough to take that step. I did make a mental note to talk with Neena about it, hoping that she might be able to persuade her aunt and uncle to consider the option.

I might have cancelled the trip altogether had I talked first to Glenn, who recounted her own horror stories of taking her kids to Disney, as a single parent. But, my friend Marion put it best, "Disney is hell!" I thought it was just me. What a relief. Moral of the story -- the things on your bucket list, like the things of life, do not always turn out the way you expect. However, you can't know that, unless you're game enough to try them.

No. 2 on my list was my intention to go to the Sundance Film Festival -- that premier showcase for independent films that's held annually in Park City, Utah. I had been a television production major at Emerson College and I had always loved the video classes I took there, especially film criticism. There's hardly a movie I watch, without putting on my critic's hat, and interpreting the symbolism and meaning behind everything obvious. Some may find that an annoying quirk. So, don't watch the movie with me, then.

At Emerson, Dale Schwartz, the college film critic, lived on the floor where I was Resident Assistant, during my junior and senior years. He managed to get loads of free film passes and often asked me to go along. I never said no, and got to see more movie openings than at any other time in my life.

Sundance was a fantasy to me then, though oddly enough, this would have been an ideal place for Matthew and me to vacation. Matthew was a film major at Emerson and a love of film is something we'd always had in common. It made sense that we would have wanted to share Sundance, and we had actually mentioned it, but neither of us ever took the initiative to plan a visit.

My friend Patrick helped me to fulfill this second goal on my bucket list. Off we went to Park City, where I discovered it's quite difficult to get advance tickets to films. However, the people at Sundance assured me that films we would see. Lo and behold, we did. Twice, while boarding a bus to the theater we'd decided upon, hoping to be able to get in, we were given passes by people who wouldn't be seeing that particular film.

One of the films that really touched me was *Away from Her,* a heart-wrenching story about a woman beginning to suffer from Alzheimer's and the pain her husband goes through in, ultimately, putting her in a nursing home. While there, she becomes the loving caretaker of another patient. The husband meets the wife of this man and they start a relationship based on both of their circumstances and the loneliness each feels. After the film, we heard from the young Canadian director, producers and an actor or two. I just loved it.

Crazy Love was a documentary about just that -- a crazy kind of love between a man who, upon hearing his ex-girlfriend is engaged, hires someone to throw lye in her face, which blinded her. Fast-forward 30 years, the girlfriend's engagement long since broken off, and he is divorced from his former wife. Upon his release from prison, he pursues his victim romantically and, ultimately, they marry. True story. The couple appeared on the Mike Douglas television show and numerous other shows in the 1970s to discuss this crazy love. The documentary did a brilliant job illustrating just how unpredictable life can be -- not that I needed to hear too much to convince me about that.

With two items accomplished, I began to think about how there are some friends in life, regardless of how long you've known them, or how long it's been between visits, with whom you can easily pick up the pieces, as if no time has passed at all. Being with those friends was, naturally, on my bucket list.

Abigail and Sean were my old neighbors on Hill Street from 1990 to 1994. We had dinner parties and neighborhood get-togethers and saw each other quite often. This was during the time when I, so desperately, wanted children, and couldn't conceive. Sean traveled a lot and Matthew worked long hours, so Abigail and I naturally bonded -- especially on our trips to Bloomingdales and Saks, T.J. Maxx, Homegoods and Marshalls.

Abigail is a stunning blonde and a true girlie-girl. No matter what she wears, she looks put together. You know the type. I'm guessing that everyone has that one friend who, regardless of the chaos in her life, looks and acts like she's got life wrapped up in a pretty little package. When you entered Abigail's house, music was playing, candles were lit and wonderful smells wafted from the kitchen. She was a throwback to days gone by, in a good way. There was something so lovely about Abigail that made me want to be around her more, not less. Which is why it was devastating for me, when she and Sean left the U.S. to head back home to the United Kingdom in 2000.

Since she'd been gone, I'd seen her twice. Once in Grand Central Station in New York City, when we shared a great lunch, two bottles of wine and nonstop conversation lamenting our lives, marriages, the pressures of parenting -- you get the picture. Our other visit occurred when she came to the States for some surgery. We didn't skip a beat in our conversation when I visited her during her recovery in Boston.

Every memory I have of Abigail is a sweet one. I could listen to her beautiful British accent for days and that, in fact, was exactly what I wanted to do. Therefore, in 2007, I decided that what the "doctor" ordered was for me to get some Abigail time. I was secretly relieved that she was working until noon the day I arrived, so that I could attempt to look presentable. Up to that point, I cared little about how I looked on the outside. The scars from my ordeal had left their mark physically and emotionally, I suppose. I was just so happy to see Abigail, her husband Sean and their sons, Andrew and Gabe.

A day or two later, Abigail sat me down at the local pub and said flat out, "It's about the way you look. It's like you don't care anymore and, Nancy, that is just not you. You need your brows waxed and could use some makeup. I can't remember ever seeing you without your hair blown out and styled. It's like you aren't you anymore. You're letting yourself go and you cannot do that now. You just can't, Nancy."

Only a true friend can, and will, say that to you. What had tipped her off? The fact that I had been wearing the same sweat suit since the day I arrived in England?

Now, if it was someone else saying that, I might have wanted to kick her in the butt, however, it hit me that she was right. I had allowed myself to slip into a funk. If a true friend is going to muster up the courage to be brutally honest, you know you need to take drastic measures. I got my brows and hair done, almost immediately, and replaced the sweat suit with not quite the little black dress, but at least the sweat suit alternative. I got up every day and put on makeup, whether I was leaving the house or not.

Life Lesson #39:

We get back what we project out into the world. The image we send out is our responsibility and is how people see us. If someone you know is in a funk, take her shopping or to the salon. Get a mani or pedi or better yet, both. Give her the gentle kick of a friend to get out there and get it together.

Abigail is the one who made me re-emerge into the world of giving a shit about things, that were seemingly unimportant to me at the time. She helped me to find my way to some semblance of normal -- caring about things that had been put on the back burner, when life and death were the only options on the table. When I returned home, my support group of Women with Controlling Partners couldn't have been more pleased to see me show up in something other than velour or fleece!

That third item on my bucket list gave me the inspiration I needed to fulfill so many of the other goals I wanted to attain. While some items, like Disney, don't go quite the way you intend, others, like this trip to England, go above and beyond your expectations. But, that's Abigail for you.

Having gotten some of the wanderlust out of my system, I began to think that there's no place like home. Dorothy sure got that right -- and I had been without one for quite a while. Though, buying a home was no drop-in-the-bucket financially, it was an absolute "must add" to my bucket list. The divorce dust had settled and I knew what kind of money I could afford to spend. Now, I could determine the kind of home I could purchase. Ideally, I wanted a home in the same school district we were currently living, so my two youngest wouldn't have to deal with being the new kids at school. They had already been through enough change for a couple of lifetimes.

J.C., my realtor friend, was right there to help me. I knew what I wanted and, ironically, a house that I fell in love with was one that Matthew ended up buying. Even more ironic, I made an offer on a house that I thought would be more ideal for him than me. Why? There are really good reasons for my seeming madness. Though I felt the house I chose was completely nondescript and devoid of character, it offered a few essentials. It was on a cul-de-sac in a great neighborhood; it had four bedrooms, so each of my kids could have their own, if they wanted, and it had two and one-half baths -- a must for a household with three kids.

Nevertheless, the essential quality that really drew me to this house was the fact that I knew I could make it my own. There was no one else's footprint on it, no previous owner's taste or influence to steer me in a predetermined direction. I could build a solid foundation for my new life, on a clean slate. Opening the door to my house is a physical reminder that I am living the life I have chosen, on my own terms and in my own home.

As I got comfortable in my new home, I became increasingly aware of how much I still loved -- and lived in -- my sweats and pajamas. I love my comfy cozies, okay? I don't think there's anything wrong with that. But I confess that, after a few lectures from Susan and Abigail about my appearance -- combined with the positive response I'd received, after making a minor attempt at pulling myself together for my support group meetings -- I was warming up to the concept of dropping the sweats for another "uniform," as it were, when I went out of the house. Therefore, that would make this No. 6 on my bucket of goals.

After buying a house and traveling to another country, getting out of sweats for good wasn't really that difficult, after all. The overwhelmingly positive response I had received, after returning from England and making an effort to put on "real" clothes and makeup, was just the intervention I needed to get back on the road to a fashion recovery.

It was good.

Life Lesson #40:

Start off with some great-fitting jeans. Nothing makes you feel better about your body than a pair of jeans that actually fit right. Next, black and white long and short sleeve T-shirts are a must. A great black dress is ideal -- thank God for

Spanx, that have a high waist, and were amazing at hiding my post-transplant scars. They are the perfect accompaniment, when wearing a sexy black satin dress.

To be honest, for a while I did do a double-take, whenever I caught a glimpse of myself in a mirror. Who was that slight, slim, trim person? It was, in fact, me --though a skinnier (but physically weaker) version. I have to say, I now understand the distorted body image that anorexics and bulimics believe about themselves. I continued to shop as though I was still a size 10 -- not a size 2. It was bizarre to think that the body image that I'd associated with myself for decades had changed overnight, whether I was seeing it in a fitting room or the privacy of my own home.

Fortunately, I did get over that and love that I have it goin' on!

There were so many physical goals to fulfill, but there was one very emotional bucket list item I had to conquer. I wanted to fall in love, again. The fact that I ended up fulfilling this goal with the man who introduced me to Rolfing, makes me wonder, *"What was I thinking?"* How could I love a man who recommended I do that? However, I'm the one who followed through with it!

Don't get me wrong. Falling in love is wonderful, but it does come with hazards -- sometimes, with flashing lights and sirens. Remember -- this was the same man that I managed to end up in the Emergency Room with, due to the lodged contraceptive device in my va-jay-jay! Ladies (and gentlemen) -- love hurts, don't kid yourself.

Life Lesson #41:

It really is better to have loved and lost than never to have loved at all, as corny as that may sound. The blessing in all of it was that I learned it was possible to love again -- even though he wasn't "the one." I suddenly felt hope that love springs eternal and that it could happen for me, again, some day. For that, I am forever grateful.

In time, I discovered there were more reasons to believe that he was not the one for me. Nevertheless, I'm glad I learned that early in the relationship. I had spent more than enough time on an ill-fated romance. In the case of my ex-husband, however, it was time well spent, as I walked away with three beautiful children, who I would not have had without him.

Despite my negative experiences looking for love in all the wrong places -- like a bar -- I did meet my current beau in just such a place. The lounge at Serafina's, one of my favorite local restaurants, is where I met Evan. I'd gone out for drinks with friends, just to have a relaxing evening and catch up on girl talk. I guess it's true that love -- or at least, really strong attraction -- strikes when you least expect it.

Evan and his friend were sitting just to my left, and I couldn't help but notice his appearance. Tall, silver-haired, well dressed -- he reminded me of the straight version of Tim Gunn, who I just love.

The men smiled and acknowledged us, and we all went back to our own conversations. But, as these things go, Evan and I remained very aware of one another, exchanging occasional glances and smiles that quickly led to an animated and very comfortable conversation. This had the potential to be very interesting! By the end of the evening, I'd given him my phone number and left the restaurant feeling pretty confident that he'd call.

Yes, Evan did call -- on Friday, to ask if he could take me to dinner on Saturday.

Being the lady that I am, I declined his invitation and suggested, instead, that we meet the following week. No way was I about to appear dateless -- and desperate -- on a 24-hour notice.

Our first date went well. I really liked Evan and felt that the interest was mutual. Nevertheless, he continued to call on short notice to ask me out, so I had to enforce the "Wednesday rule" upon him. If you're not familiar with it, that's the rule that says a man can't call a woman for a Saturday date any later than Wednesday. It took some time, but he finally got it.

Like me, Evan is divorced; unlike me, he has one adult daughter. Unlike me, he's also almost neurotically cautious about relationships. We dated for quite some time before we were intimate, because he believes that it should take a long time to get to know someone. I found that unusual for a man, and actually started dating other people, while Evan took his time feeling comfortable enough to commit to me. In fact, I offered to be his love coach!

He is a very interesting man, though, and pretty damn successful, but he wouldn't tell you that. He has very high self-expectations and is quite hard on himself. Evan owns dozens of rental properties; in addition to that, he holds a full-time position with a major pharmaceutical corporation. Most people would consider themselves set with his income and great benefits.

Life Lesson #42:

Personal success and satisfaction are unique to every individual. You can think a man or woman has it all, while that same someone sees their life as a disappointment.

Although we're very close, after more than three years together, in a way, I think that Evan just may be a consummate bachelor. Right now, I enjoy his company and his loyalty and sentimental nature. My kids like him and he's very good to them. We have fun together. I've learned enough, through the years, to understand that love can't always be a thunderbolt. Not every relationship is a whirlwind, and that's a good thing. I had the whirlwind with Marcus, and when I finally stopped spinning, found myself alone and unhappy. Maybe, this nice, calm relationship with Evan is just what I need right now. Maybe, it's better to think that it might not be forever; that way, I won't be taken by surprise, if it isn't.

Despite my love of nice things and my desire to make the best appearance, there is one area in which I'm not at all compelled to have the newest, prettiest model. I am not a "car person," in spite of Matthew's attorney referring to me, as the Imelda Marcos -- the infamous, financially extravagant politician in the Philippines -- of the auto industry. Imelda became infamous for owning more than 2,000 pairs of shoes. For me, buying a vehicle was a necessity on my list of things I needed to do. After my car was sold out from under me -- while I was in a coma, in case I never mentioned that -- I managed to recoup some funds to buy myself a new vehicle. Not the snazzy Mercedes convertible that would be on most people's bucket lists, I'll bet. Nope, I opted for the mini-van. It's not sexy, but it's a cost-effective and practical vehicle -- just like sensible shoes. Go buy one. That's my plug to help revive the automobile industry.

Though I sense a mid-life crisis could come on and I'll get that red Mercedes, yet, until then I need a boat-on-wheels to drive my kids (and their entourage) to and from various events and activities, and let's not forget the mall.

I've already devoted an entire chapter to this next major goal of my new life. I wanted to make new friends. The shakedown of my friendships was somewhat surreal and disheartening, but in the end, I have to look at it as a blessing. It hurts so good to see who your friends are -- and who they are not.

While some appeared to be by my side, when I lay unconscious in a Critical Care Unit, soon after I awoke they were nowhere to be found. That is, unless you consider their daily delivery of messages to my ex-husband, as well as a house-warming gift of cookies the day we moved out of our marital home, as signs of friendship. Oddly, some of them found their way to my new house on moving day -- not to be there for moral support, but to be aware about what was going down.   True colors do not always form a beautiful rainbow.

Life Lesson #43:

I know now who has always been my friend, who I want to be my friend and how to be a friend to others. I've made new friends, carefully and deliberately, and with them, my bucket runneth over.

Apparently, though, I haven't mastered the trip thing, all that well. Not sure what I was thinking here, and without my friend Connie from my support group coming along, my bucket-list trip to Nantucket for a week might have proved impossible.

This trip happened two years after my illness, and just getting there was nothing short of a miracle. Connie and I hired two teenage girls to assist with our five children, ranging in ages from 7 to 12. In the end, the girls turned out to be more work than help. Further complicating matters, was the issue of Connie's boyfriend, Edward, courtesy of 8-minute dating, who showed up just in time for a harbor cruise gone awry.

Edward was so not right for her. While on our harbor cruise, we got into a conversation with a lovely older woman, who asked how long we had all been married. Marcus was still in the mix then, and we were getting along quite well at the time.

We laughed and explained our statuses and situations, about which the woman said, *"I should have done what you did, years ago."* She was married for 50 years and said that she'd only had about three years of happiness in her entire marriage -- combined. How sad. Even sadder, her husband was sitting on the deck right above her -- and heard every word!

Life Lesson #44:
I guess it is true that, if everyone put all their problems in a pot and had to pick one, we would all choose the same problems we placed there. I thought my divorce was the last thing I wanted, but really, this woman's unfulfilling marriage seemed like 50 wasted years to me.
So much worse than divorce.

Edward, who was totally buzzed before he even got on the ship, became incensed when this woman observed that Marcus and I seemed like a good couple, while he and Connie did not seem to belong together. Suffice it to say, the two of them fought the entire evening, and then acted like lovebirds the next day. It was so uncomfortable to watch.

My 12-year-old was in rare form on this trip, suffering from a hormonal imbalance called adolescence, which made for an interesting but challenging vacation. Catherine had a major meltdown at one point, screaming that I was the worst mother in the world and, in fact, not her real mother, and that she was going to call all of her friends and tell them what a bad mother I was. I called her bluff by agreeing to do her dirty work of calling her friends myself, and that's where the episode ended. I was still too weak for all this drama and very glad Connie was there to help. However, at least, I had accomplished another goal.

So, that was my list. I am happy and proud to say that I crossed off each, and every one, of those 10 items. What I discovered is that not every single thing for which I wished or dreamed, fulfilled my expectations.

At the end of the day, I think the moral of the bucket list is to just go ahead and make one. Whatever drives you to do it -- sickness, divorce, depression, boredom -- just go ahead and make one. I think, maybe, the point is to simply have some expectations and desires. That's what gets us all through the day, the night, the month, the year. Looking forward to things is what life is all about. Then have the determination to follow through and see how many goals you can achieve.

CHAPTER 10

BACK IN THE HIGH LIFE AGAIN

Making and completing my bucket list is probably -- no, definitely -- one of the best things I've ever done. After the physical and emotional trauma of my illness and divorce, it was absolutely life affirming to ponder what I really wanted to do, and then actually do it. I think one of the most positive aspects of the entire undertaking is that each, and every one, of the items on the list was *mine*. I'm the one who made the decisions to go to Disney, visit my friends in England, buy a new home, and pursue the rest of my goals. No one told me that I had to do any of those things and I didn't do a single one of them, against my will.

During my marriage, my husband constantly overshadowed me with his charm, wit and overbearing personality. He filled the room with words, so much so, that few people heard me speak. He was exhausting and too much with whom to compete. When he left, I thought I'd lost it all, but learned that I had so much more, yet to lose. Since I have been healthy, I am back to the person I used to be -- before the illness, before Matthew -- strong, frank, independent and funny.

For the first time, since I married, people actually notice who I am. *"You know, you're funny,"* they say, somewhat surprised. No kidding!

I've learned more about myself since the divorce and resolution of my health issues, than I ever knew before. Knowing who you are gives you such a sense of control. It has made me feel like a grown-up.

Now, feeling like a grown-up, and really being one, are not necessarily one and the same. Nevertheless, after having gone through several lifetimes' worth of my own personal hell, I knew that a grown-up I must be. I decided to take that feeling of control and run with it, embracing it as fully as I did with my recovered health, and my precious children. Barring another unforeseen illness, I became determined that the rest of my life will truly be mine, created by me and lived on my terms.

The first thing I knew -- without question -- was that a primary element of my new life had to be an attitude of gratitude. Oh God, I'd surely been through hell, but I had come out on the other side -- back to the world, to my children and my life. As hard and truly painful as the last five years have been, I am grateful to have survived, and survived well.

I am also grateful for all of the lessons I've learned throughout the ordeal. However, I am far from ready for canonization. Trust me, as grateful as I am for all that I have, I still do a lot of the things that I silently swore I'd never do again, during the times I was fighting so hard to get my kids back, struggling to breathe on my own, or wishing I could drive a car. I yell at my kids, send them to their rooms or ask them to just leave me alone for a few minutes, when I've had enough. I don't praise God for every breath I take, though I vowed I would when coming off that trach. I curse while I sit in traffic, and wish I didn't have to drive the kids to so many places, because sometimes I feel like I live in that damn car. I get cranky, when I have to clean the house. While I was throwing up, bald and on a feeding tube, I would have given just about anything to look "normal" -- forget pretty or fashionable. I promised myself that if, and when, I got well, I would never again feel inadequate in my physical appearance. Then, just a couple of measly years later, I let some woman at a speed-dating interview make me feel lacking in self-worth and self-conscious.

The thing is, though, this is really how I know that I've made a full recovery from the illness and from my divorce. The little things that I wished then were my only problems, are now my biggest problems.

Nevertheless, what had once been important to me -- the big house, the fancy life -- I realized were not important at all. While I'd thought the 6,000-square-foot house mattered, I'd been blind to the reality of what was happening to the family living inside it.

Now, in a house which is one-third the size of my previous abode, lives a happy family. Savanah, Nathan, Catherine and I don't need all the trappings of our old life. What we need is right inside my cozy house -- love, warmth, and happiness -- mixed with chaos, sibling rivalry, and more stuff than with which we know what to do. We are an incredibly normal family. We have a real home. We are happy.

Moving to a smaller house carries its own set of lessons. While it might seem obvious that a smaller house will logically hold fewer possessions, it's really not so simple. You'd be surprised at the amount of crap from which we're all unwilling or afraid to part. As George Carlin said, *"A house is just a pile of stuff with a cover on it."* Ain't that the truth?

Although happy in my new home and ecstatic to have my kids living with me, I began to realize, at some point, that we were surrounded by just too damn much stuff. The basement was full to the rafters with all manner of junk that I, finally, realized was completely non-essential.

Life Lesson #45:

Let's face it, if you haven't looked for an item, haven't missed it or wondered where it was in the last year, chances are pretty good that you don't need the damn thing. The motto at my local five-and-dime store, right here in West Concord, is, "If we don't have it, you don't need it." So true.

So, we began weeding through and getting rid of all that unnecessary stuff. It wasn't easy, at first. Every item seemed to have a life of its own -- a precious memory attached to it. But, I started to realize another lesson. Those memories exist within me, and I shouldn't need a prompt to remind me of them. I don't need Nathan's old bike to picture him riding it, trying so hard to keep from wobbling; or the girls' dollhouse to see them lovingly arranging its tiny furniture in the minute spaces.

No, I own those memories. They are part of the fabric of my heart. As long as I have memory, I'll have those images and experiences with me. Once my mind starts to get mushy, the kids can show me pictures to remind me.

There is, actually, a delicious irony to this cleaning project. In our old house, the basement leaked, and I swear that the mildew and muck crept upward, infecting all of us with an incipient decay. In my new home, the uncluttered basement has made me see the rest of the house with fresh eyes. This time, what emanates from the basement is fresh air, the lightness and weightlessness of being freed from the albatross of too much stuff.

Life Lesson #46:
Things do not make you happy, people make you happy; moments make you happy.

The basement project has since progressed throughout the house. Once I learned to let go of things that we hadn't used in a long time, it became easier to look more objectively at the things that make up our everyday life. I'm amazed at how infrequently I really thought about an item, about whether we needed it or had simply become accustomed to seeing it in its regular place.

You'd be surprised by how differently you feel when you simply stop and look. Take a good look around the room that you're in right now. Do you really *see* anything, or do you just recognize each object as one of your possessions, in its proper place? Come on, fess up, when is the last time you switched out the books on your shelf, or rearranged those little doo-dads on the kitchen windowsill? Making some simple changes can refresh the energy in a room, making it feel like a completely new space.

As much as I love my work, if I had it to do all over again, I'd probably pursue a career in interior design. I guess, the same principles that I've learned from my near-death experience can be applied to decorating and design, as well. Accentuate the positive, eliminate the negative; put the focus on the two or three pieces that really make a statement, that mean something on a deeper level. Everything else is a backdrop.

I really believe in the principles of *feng shui*, how the way we organize and decorate our homes, can help us lead prosperous and healthy lives by blocking negative energies. It's been interesting to rearrange the things in my home with those principles in mind. Not only does the place look great, but also, I swear it's had a definite effect on me, which is more or less the entire point. I feel so much more content; everything is in its place and all is right with the world. Well, all is right with my home; I'm still working on the rest of the world.

Another lesson I've learned is that when you come upon a great idea, stick with it. If creating and fulfilling my bucket list had such a positive effect on my life, why not do it, again? After learning some harsh lessons about fear and hopelessness, I believe, wholeheartedly, in looking forward -- not to the past. Making plans helped get me through my long recovery, although there were many times when the list seemed more like a collection of fantasies, which would never come true.

Now that I'm well, inside and out, I've discovered that making a bucket list is an entirely different proposition than my first. The term "bucket list" came from a 2007 American film in which Jack Nicholson and Morgan Freeman play two terminally ill men. They embark on a road trip with a wish list of things to do "before they kick the bucket." This time, I'm creating my list with a whole new attitude. The goals I put on my list are there because they will fulfill and enrich my life and the lives of those around me -- not just because I want to be able to say I did them, before I die.

The first thing I'd like to do is invest in real estate. I'm not aiming for Donald Trump's empire; I'd just like to buy a little house in Concord that I could manage as a rental. It would be a great way to ensure some additional income for the future. The good news is that I can learn from a master, since Evan is quite the real estate baron. I think that, with his guidance, I could find an affordable place, and with my interest in design, I'd be happy with a fixer-upper. In fact, I would prefer an older house that I can transform.

I figure I did a pretty good job fixing up the shell that houses my soul, from bottom to top, from deep inside to the parts on the surface that everyone can see. A physical dwelling, in need of an overhaul, is right up my alley. In fact, right now, I'm keeping an eye on a particular house, that looks like a starving dog had been living in the basement and was trying to scratch and claw his way out. Some wonder why I would want to buy a house that is so problematic, but that's precisely why. A great songwriter once wrote, *"There are no problems, only solutions."*

That's how I look at business, as well. As CEO of my own company and a well-known, well-traveled marketing consultant, the things I've experienced in my personal life have helped me to grow into a better businesswoman. I have more clarity about my own value and worth, and my ability to communicate that to clients and corporations, alike.

Life Lesson #47:

Everything that goes before you in your life, helps you accomplish goals where you find yourself, now.

Many people are uncomfortable with the marketing aspect of business. They are afraid of rejection, and hey, who can blame them? Rejection, whether personal or professional, isn't fun. In managing my health, my family and my home, I've learned a good deal about how similar personal life and business, really are.

In both cases, dealing with the decision-maker is the only way to get anything done. In both cases, being selfishly motivated doesn't work; to strike a deal and a long-standing relationship, things need to be win-win for all parties involved. Both personal life and business are about making and maintaining personal connections with people. Sometimes, that requires a good deal of perseverance.

One story, about that somewhat challenging trait, has always struck a chord with me. Tony Robbins, the great motivational speaker, told a story about a guy named Chet Holmes, who sent him something via email or regular mail every single week for ten years. That's how badly this man wanted to work with Robbins and, eventually, Robbins determined that type of commitment and perseverance should be recognized. They have since worked on projects together. That theme of perseverance, of not giving up, is huge.

Life Lesson #48:

One of the best -- and easiest -- ways to make and maintain connections is to treat people the way you want to be treated. You don't need a Master's Degree in Business Administration to figure that one out.

My next goal is important on a couple of levels. I want to take my children to China. That might seem perfectly natural, since it's the country where Savanah and Catherine were born. Interestingly, though, the girls really aren't very interested. They are so utterly American, despite their Asian roots. I guess, that's the real sign that they feel no different from the rest of our family, which was my goal from the moment they both came into my life. Unlike his sisters, Nathan has written about his desire to "go to China to learn more about the most populated country in the world and to eat a lot of fish and frogs." Maybe, he was Chinese in a past life, as I feel I might have been.

Aside from the familial connection, though, I'm very interested in China's emerging position as a superpower, that may well change the global economy and, perhaps, surpass the United States on a number of levels. I think it's important for my kids to understand the nation that will most likely have a serious impact on their futures.

Back on the home front, I want to make some cosmetic changes to my house. I love the cozy little English-cottage look and think a picket fence around my yard, along with a cupola and weathervane on the garage, would look perfect. The house can use a new roof, so if I'm going to do that -- what the heck, I may as well complete the look. I can just picture my pretty house and garden. I have some great ideas, but I would, definitely, hire a contractor to help me flesh them out. Lowe's and Home Depot, here I come!

Since I love the English-cottage style, it makes sense to go to England for first-hand inspiration. Honestly, though, my real reason for wanting to visit England is to see Abigail, again. My last trip was so positive and uplifting -- I came home a new person -- thanks to Abigail's honest concern and friendship. I'm sure she could give me some current tips for updating my look, again. I've got lots of frequent flier miles; surely there are enough for a round-trip ticket. I, also, have a feeling that Abigail might be needing me now, too. You know how you just have that connection with certain friends? Sometimes, you don't need anything concrete to let you know that it's time to get together; you can simply feel it. That's it -- tomorrow I'm buying an international calling card and phoning Abigail.

Right after the phone call, we'll go to my favorite Chinese restaurant. I've slaved away one time too many for my annual Chinese New Year's party, and in the end, I probably don't have to tell you -- it's a drag. Do you ever think, when you attend a great party at someone's house, about how that person feels the day after? Maybe, you've been the party-thrower yourself, so you know the feeling first-hand. Everyone has a great time, and I spend the next two days drinking massive amounts of coffee and thinking to myself, "I'll never do that again." Not good.

This year, I'm cutting a deal with a Chinese restaurant to not only cater, but serve and clean up, as well. Far from being extravagant, this ties in, quite nicely, with my goal of downsizing and simplifying (my workload) and being grateful for and enjoying life (and my guests).

Deeply flawed as I am, my bucket list would not be complete without a couple of physical accoutrements. I want to get my two front teeth straightened and a little plastic surgery, while I'm at it. It's my secret as to which part of my body gets the remodeling!

While I'm being a tad vain, I'm going to go ahead and add a new set of wheels with a vanity plate. The vanity plate, well, that's the easy part. While I continue to profess that I'm not a car person, a new car made it onto my Top 10 List twice, so maybe, I'm still learning a thing or two about myself on this journey. I sure hope so! I might as well enjoy the ride in a convertible, don't you think?

This next item on my bucket list is partially complete. One of the turning points in my life, after I'd finally gotten it back, was making the decision to write my story and hire writers to do it. I've got my voice back now and more tales to recount than one person should ever be privileged to tell, but somehow, I knew I had to take a step away from it. Believe me, when I read back on the times of my life, I can barely fathom that all this has happened to one person. To me. However, the truth is stranger than fiction, as they say.

In the end, I did the best I could with what I had to work. I didn't go through all of it gracefully. I wasn't always brave. I didn't experience the traumatic events of my life with a purposeful sense that they would give me insight into myself, as a person. I lost my marriage, my health, my kids and my voice. Stripped naked. In return, I got a transplant, truth and a life transformation.

I am one of the lucky ones, who got to see her life flash before her very eyes and got the opportunity to rewind, slow it down and edit the pieces that, ultimately, didn't work with her life's story.

That doesn't happen every day -- thank the good Lord.

Life Lesson #49:

Sometimes the worst thing that can happen becomes the best thing that will ever happen to you.

EPILOGUE

GIFTS FROM BEING AN ORGAN RECIPIENT

There have been so many gifts I've been the grateful recipient of, because of the greatest gift I've been given -- a second chance at life -- thanks to the kindness of a complete stranger.

First off, I had the pleasure of meeting the parents and children of my organ donor when I took my son to Appalachia, VA to meet them. While there, I had the honor of speaking at a public event to celebrate my donor's life, as well as my survival. It was one of those life-altering and memorable events. I am grateful to dedicate this book to my organ donor and to remain in touch with her family.

I connected with the acting chairman of Blue Cross Blue Shield, my insurance provider, and thanked him for the experience I had with my coverage from BCBS during my illness. He, graciously, connected me with the corporate marketing department. Subsequently, I was featured, along with my three children, in an advertisement about my experience as an organ recipient. The ads ran over four months and I became a local "celeb" as a result. I heard from people I hadn't heard from in years. My children and I are now proud carrying Screen Actor's Guild (SAG) members. Most importantly, it was an amazing forum to share my experience as an organ recipient.

I have appeared on numerous morning television shows to promote Donate Life and the month of April, as organ donation month. I have been blessed to share my story and offer the truth about organ donation. I was an organ donor myself, and one of the most amazing fears I hear from people, is the anxiety they have about not being saved if they are an organ donor. I can tell you, first-hand, that is NOT the case.

In May of 2010, I attended Speakers, Authors Networking Group (SANG) headed by Larry Benet. I was on the fence about attending but, in my gut, I felt I should. I am glad I went and I've formed some of the most amazing relationships, as a result. While there, I reconnected with Sandra Yancey, the founder of eWomenNetwork. Larry created an environment at SANG, whereby we could all ask for help with something we needed. Sandra stood up and asked if anyone was familiar with a non-profit that assisted with organ donation. I approached her, during the break, and gave her the name of Donate Life. I followed-up with her when I returned home, and she asked me to speak at the eWomenNetwork convention in 2011, in Dallas, TX.

I took the main stage during the luncheon and shared my story of being an organ recipient, along with the impact it had on my life, and that of my family. I showed the photos of me that are on the back cover of this book, as a symbol to all women and men in the audience, that comebacks are very possible. A board member, of Donate Life, also spoke about the need for living and deceased organ donors and, again, it was another amazing moment I might never have had without the gift of being a recipient. The big surprise came when Donate Life's board member was describing what the 2012 Donate Life float's theme would be -- One More Day. Sandra then pulled me in front of the audience and told me that eWomenNetwork would be sponsoring me as one the 2012 float riders in the Rose Bowl Parade -- and I would be holding a flora-graph of my donor's beautiful face! I was stunned and overwhelmed by the generosity of this gift.

As a Christmas gift to my children and parents, I took everyone to California for a vacation, starting in Santa Monica, and then going to Pasadena for the Rose Bowl Parade. There were lovely dinners, brunches and events for all, to meet with other families of organ donors, along with the recipients, like myself. Amazing.

We toured the floats being made, which were breathtaking. It's one of those things I think should be on everyone's bucket list. During the judging session (the day before the actual parade on January 1, 2012), the judges slowly circled our float as the theme song -- *100 Years*, by Five for Fighting -- played in the background. As the judging session neared an end, the judges began to ask us if we were organ recipients or relatives of donors. Grown men were crying as they heard our stories.

One of the float riders was a mother of an 8-year-old girl, who was shot at Gabby Gifford's rally in Arizona.

My dad was an emotional mess at the end of the session and, for what was the first time in my life that I remember, said how proud he was of me. Deep down, I'm sure I knew he was, but it was a wonderful thing to hear at that moment. I am so grateful for the experience, and that I could share it with my three children, along with my parents.

The day of the Rose Bowl Parade was surreal -- in the best sense of the word. We gathered in the hotel lobby at 5am, and loaded a bus to where the floats had been lined up, in the order that we would float throughout Pasadena. As we were stepping onto the float, people were gathering on their lawns and sidewalks, in front of us. When the people realized what our float was about, we received an overwhelming response from them. Many people told us stories of their own family members, who had passed on and were organ donors. They wanted to know how their loved one could be recognized on the float. It was such an emotional ride, which lasted a couple of hours, while waving to the crowd, as we held the flora-graphs of our respective donors.

It was, again, a once in a lifetime experience that I'll be forever changed and grateful for. When I returned home, I was able to do more local television interviews about my experience as a float rider. I was emotionally exhausted, but gained lifetime memories with my family, as a result.

After I got over the shock of my son Nathan's tab at the bar in the hotel -- $87.00 spent on "Coca-Colas," it was a *more* than memorable experience.

ABOUT THE AUTHOR

Nancy Michaels is CEO and Founder of Grow Your Business Network, the place where business grows up. Coined as "America's #1 Fortune 500 Consultant" Nancy is a globally recognized business development coach, speaker, and consultant to both large and small business owners and companies targeting women. Her consulting and marketing programs have a proven track record of enabling companies to generate unique marketing, sales and relationship propositions with the focus on sustainable growth and transformation. Satisfied clients like Office Depot, Walmart, UPS, Xerox, Constant Contact, Staples, HP and many others have benefited by Nancy's tried and true methods for igniting results and attaining goals. She has consulted, spoken and taught in 42 states to more than 100,000 entrepreneurs.

Nancy has authored five books including *Perfecting Your Pitch*, *Off The Wall Marketing Ideas*, *How To Be A Big Fish In Any Pond*, *Media Madness*, and *A to Z to Visibility*. She has been featured in numerous business publications such as *Entrepreneur* magazine, *US News and World Report*, *Business Week*, and *Fortune Small Business*. To learn more about Nancy, please visit www.nancymichaels.com.

In the spring of 2005, Nancy became very ill and underwent a liver transplant due to liver failure. She is the grateful recipient of a donor liver.

Find out how you can become a donor at organdonor.gov and donatelife.net

www.ingramcontent.com/pod-product-compliance
Lightning Source LLC
LaVergne TN
LVHW020926090426
835512LV00020B/3227